Coordinating design and technology across the primary school

THE SUBJECT LEADER'S HANDBOOKS

Series Editor: Mike Harrison, Centre for Primary Education, School of Education, The University of Manchester, Oxford Road, Manchester, M13 9DP

Coordinating mathematics across the primary school
Tony Brown

Coordinating English at Key Stage 1
Mick Waters and Tony Martin

Coordinating English at Key Stage 2
Mick Waters and Tony Martin

Coordinating science across the primary school
Lynn D. Newton and Douglas P. Newton

Coordinating information and communications technology across the primary school
Mike Harrison

Coordinating art across the primary school
Judith Piotrowski, Robert Clements and Ivy Roberts

Coordinating design and technology across the primary school
Alan Cross

Coordinating geography across the primary school
John Halocha

Coordinating history across the primary school
Julie Davies and Jason Redmond

Coordinating music across the primary school
Sarah Hennessy

Coordinating religious education across the primary school
Derek Bastide

Coordinating physical education across the primary school
Carole Raymond

Management skills for SEN coordinators
Sylvia Phillips, Jennifer Goodwin and Rosita Heron

Building a whole school assessment policy
Mike Wintle and Mike Harrison

The curriculum coordinator and the OFSTED inspection
Phil Gadsby and Mike Harrison

Coordinating the curriculum in the smaller primary school
Mick Waters

Coordinating design and technology across the primary school

Alan Cross

FALMER PRESS
Taylor & Francis Group

UK	The Falmer Press, 1 Gunpowder Square, London, EC4A 3DE
USA	The Falmer Press, Taylor & Francis Inc., 1900 Frost Road, Suite 101, Bristol, PA 19007

First published in 1998

A catalogue record for this book is available from the British Library

ISBN 0 7507 0689 9 paper

Library of Congress Cataloging-in-Publication Data are available on request

Jacket design by Carla Turchini

Typeset in 10/14 pt Melior by
Graphicraft Typesetters Ltd., Hong Kong.

Contents

Part one
The role of the design and technology coordinator

Part two
What design and technology coordinators need to know

Part three
Whole school policies and schemes of work

Part four
Monitoring for quality

Part five
Resources for learning

List of figures

Acknowledgments

Figure 5.1, page 66: The author and Publisher would like to thank Routledge for kind permission to reproduce Figure 5.1 from Alexander, R. (1992) *Policy and Practice in Primary Education.*

Figure 6.1, page 88: The author and Publisher would like to thank David Fulton Publishers for permission to reproduce Figure 2.2 from Harlen, W. *The Teaching of Science* (first edition).

Series editor's preface

This book has been prepared for primary teachers charged with the responsibility of acting as design and technology coordinators (d&t) within their schools. It forms part of a series of new publications that set out to advise such teachers on the complex issues of improving teaching and learning through managing each element of the primary school curriculum.

Why is there a need for such a series? Most authorities recognise, after all, that the quality of the primary children's work and learning depends upon the skills of their class teacher, not in the structure of management systems, policy documents or the titles and job description of staff. Many today recognise that school improvement equates directly to the improvement of teaching so surely all tasks, other than imparting subject knowledge, are merely a distraction for the committed primary teacher.

Nothing should take teachers away from their most important role, that is, serving the best interests of the class of children in their care and this book and the others in the series do not wish to diminish that mission. However, the increasing complexity of the primary curriculum and society's expanding expectations make it very difficult for the class teacher to keep up to date with every development. Within traditional subject areas there has been an explosion of knowledge and new fields introduced such as science, technology, design, problem solving and health education, not to mention the uses of computers. These are now considered entitlements for primary children. Furthermore, we now expect all children to succeed at these studies, not just the fortunate few. All this has overwhelmed a class teacher system largely unchanged since the inception of primary schools.

Primary class teachers cannot possibly be experts in every aspect of the curriculum they are required to teach. To whom can they turn for help? It is unrealistic to assume that such support will be available from the headteacher whose responsibilities have grown ever wider since the 1988 Educational Reform Act. Constraints, including additional staff costs, and the loss of benefits from the strength and security of the class teacher system, militate against wholesale adoption of specialist or semi-specialist teaching. Help therefore has to come from exploiting the talents of teachers themselves, in a process of mutual support. Hence primary schools have chosen many and varied systems of consultancy or subject coordination which best suit the needs of their children and the current expertise of the staff.

In fact, curriculum leadership functions in primary schools have increasingly been shared with class teachers through the policy of curriculum coordination for the past twenty years, especially to improve the consistency of work in language and mathematics. Since then each school has developed their own system and the series recognises that the one each reader is part of will be a compromise between the ideal and the possible. Campbell and Neill (1994) show that by 1991 nearly nine out of every ten primary class teachers has such responsibility and the average number of subjects each was between 1.5 and 2.2 (depending on the size of school).

These are the people for whom this series sets out to help to do this part of their work. The books each deal with specific issues whilst at the same time providing an overview of general themes in the management of the subject curriculum. The term *subject leader* is used in an inclusive sense and combines the two major roles that such teachers play when they have responsibility for subjects and aspects of the primary curriculum.

The books each deal with:

- coordination — a role which emphasises: harmonising, bringing together, making links, establishing routines and common practice; and
- subject leadership — a role which emphasises: providing information, offering expertise and direction, guiding the development of the subject, and raising standards.

The purpose of the series is to give practical guidance and support to teachers, in particular what to do and how to do it. They each offer help on the production, development and review of policies and schemes of work; the organisation of resources, and developing strategies for improving the management of the subject curriculum.

Each book in the series contains material that subject managers will welcome and find useful in developing their subject expertise and in tackling problems of enthusing and motivating staff.

Each book has five parts:

1. The review and development of the different roles coordinators are asked to play.
2. Updating subject knowledge and subject pedagogical knowledge.
3. Developing and maintaining policies and schemes of work.
4. Monitoring work within the school to enhance the continuity of teaching and progression in pupils' learning.
5. Resources and contacts.

Although written primarily for teachers who are d&t coordinators, Alan Cross's book offers practical guidance and many ideas for anyone in the school who has a responsibility for the design and technology curriculum including teachers with an overall role in coordinating the whole or key stage curriculum and the deputy head and the headteacher.

In making the book easily readable, Alan has drawn upon his considerable experience as a teacher educator, researcher and OFSTED inspector with responsibility for d&t. Alan's own enthusiasm for the subject spills out into the book and makes it an enjoyable read. He has written extensively on the subject previously and his advice will be invaluable for those attempting to develop a whole-school view of progress in d&t, particularly those who are new to the job or have recently changed schools. It will help readers develop both the subject expertise they will need and the managerial perspective necessary to enthuse others.

Mike Harrison, Series Editor
January 199

Opening remarks

Primary classteachers require leadership and support to
teach design and technology as part of the primary curriculum.
Primary schools require leadership in design and technology
education to ensure coverage, balance, continuity and
progression for all children. In the primary context design
and technology is taught as part of a broad curriculum of nine
subjects, often but not always as part of an integrated topic or
theme. The response of most primary schools to the challenge
of teaching a broad and balanced curriculum is to plan
thoroughly and to delegate responsibility for the management
of subjects and aspects. This book articulates and details the
role of the coordinator for design and technology. It includes
advice about priorities and actions and considers the
development that you might encourage as a design and
technology coordinator. This is done in such a way as to
make it possible for students, teachers (including those
newly qualified and others new to the subject) to develop
professionally as they establish the needs of the school and
to begin to address them. Evaluation will be stressed as part
of the role and as a contribution to schools' systems for
monitoring and evaluating aspects of the curriculum. Perhaps
the biggest challenge for subject coordinators, particularly
those who have recently trained, is to develop and maintain
a whole-school view while maintaining a focus on individual
development by children.

The word coordinator is misleading, the word manager may be more accurate. The role varies from school to school, it is hard to imagine the headteacher managing all of the subjects, so who better to manage a subject in a primary school than a teacher in that school? It has been suggested that subjects like design and technology as part of primary education might benefit from subject experts teaching specialised lessons (Alexander et al., 1992). Subject expertise in design and technology within primary education is in short supply. We should consider the advantages of a committed primary professional, who, with support from the headteacher, can achieve much. As design and technology expertise is so scarce, primary schools may need to consider specific actions to increase experience in this area. This must focus on the coordinator, it should include the other adults working with children. Support for design and technology as part of primary education should be manifested in a number of the following ways:

- leadership from the head/senior management team;
- a place for the subject in the school development plan;
- clarity about the role of coordinator of design and technology and its relation to others in school;
- regular review of your role as coordinator;
- an annual budget sufficient for the subject;
- attention to your professional and subject INSET needs as coordinator;
- attention to the professional and subject INSET needs of the staff; and
- regular, planned, release time for you as coordinator.

Having seen that expertise in design and technology is limited in primary schools, it is important that we should make the most of what we have and build upon that actively. That is what designers and technologists (cooks, engineers, farmers, architects) do and it is certainly what we in primary education are used to!

Design and technology is a subject which is a statutory entitlement of all pupils in the United Kingdom (UK) from 5–14 years and part of the 'natural' entitlement of all pupils preparing to participate as adults in society (Eggleston, 1992). Whichever society you belong to in the twenty-first century, individuals are likely to need to be able to deploy skills and use knowledge from design and technology. Citizens will have to weigh up pros and cons in issues related to the environment and to products and services they use as consumers. They need to appreciate that science and technology often offer solutions to human problems, but that for each advantage offered there are usually corresponding disadvantages. Air travel is an example of a technology which offers much, including rapid transport of people and goods, but the disadvantages of air travel include use of land for airfields, pollution, noise and even air warfare. Science and technology almost always deliver more than the things they promise.

Primary schools are complex places. It may be relatively straightforward for a teacher to make significant changes in one classroom but those changes may never affect other classrooms. This book advocates a whole-school approach. Indeed this is the very reason that subject coordinators are identified, in order to ensure that there is a consistent, whole-school view of and approach to the subject.

This book is about management of design and technology education in primary schools and those who do that managing. It will refer to children, to their teachers and classrooms. Children are the reason for this book and their entitlement to and achievement in design and technology as part of their primary education should be the focus of the design and technology coordinator. The single aim of design and technology coordinators, and therefore the aim of this book, is raising children's attainment in design and technology and across the curriculum.

All subject coordinators should beware of being dominated by the need to provide paperwork and should constantly find opportunities to see children's design and technology work and be actively involved over a period of time in teaching and observing a wide range of children and their work.

Human beings and technology

All societies have, and in the past have had, technology. The ancient civilisations, like the Inca or the Egyptians, developed their own technology of building, clothing technology, metalwork technology, food technology, and in the case of the Egyptians, even a technology for enbalming the remains of their dead. Similar technologies are seen throughout history around the world and in the present day. All human beings have needs and aspirations, including the need for clothing, food, security, warmth, to name a few, and aspirations which include a sense of place, of self-worth, a need to express oneself. Many of these needs and aspirations are achieved through a technology. The technology of paintwork allows us to protect structures from the weather and to express complex inner feelings about humanity. These examples are as much part of the world of a six year old as an adult, as much a part of the life of a householder, teacher, plumber, artist or engineer. It is the engagement with, and response to, the 'need' and the person's ingenuity, creativity, knowledge of materials, tools and techniques that allows solutions to be found. One way to examine an individual technology is to list those things which distinguish it from other technologies. That is, all technologies have their own set of **tools**: i.e. the tools of painting technology are different from those in food technology. In the same way, each technology has its own **language**, **workplace techniques** and **practices**. Their commonality is the human being using them to solve problems.

Because so much technology derives from simple human needs for shelter, clothing, food and other basics, children are well placed to participate fully in design and technology as part of their education. All children have recent experience of dealing with and learning about these needs (see Figure I.1 — Making a house a home). As different people will often design and make different but quite acceptable solutions to a need there is much scope in design and technology for personal expression, building confidence and self-esteem. Thus design and technology as an educational experience has much to offer, firstly in its own right as a subject but also for its spin offs into other subjects and the potential it has for personal growth. It may assist you to consider examples of design and technology in your life. Think about any simple designing and making you may have been involved in whilst:

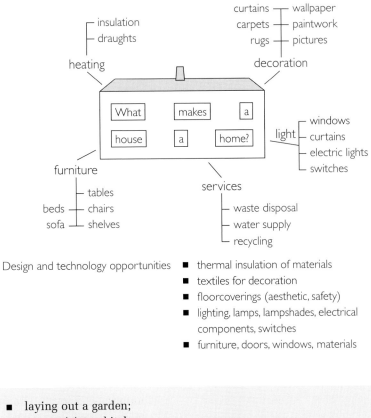

FIG I.1
Example of a theme —
What makes a house a home?

Design and technology opportunities
- thermal insulation of materials
- textiles for decoration
- floorcoverings (aesthetic, safety)
- lighting, lamps, lampshades, electrical components, switches
- furniture, doors, windows, materials

- laying out a garden;
- reorganising a kitchen;
- decorating a house;
- developing an area in school;
- preparing a sports field or equipment; or
- setting up a TV, video or computer.

Design and technology education

Design and technology is an unusual subject in that it was invented as part of the National Curriculum. Prior to the 1990 (DES) orders for technology we had growing but only sporadic implementation of Craft, Design and Technology (CDT) in the primary years. Where it occurred in primary education, design and make activities were included as part of primary topics or themes. As such, the subject was itself designed and made in 1990 and to an extent is now being evaluated. The evaluation has already seen several steps and rewrites in the form of new versions produced for consultation (DfE, 1992; NCC, 1993;

SCAA, 1994) and the latest, post-Dearing (Dearing, 1993) version (DfE, 1995) which will no doubt be superseded. The 'evolution' appears to have been driven more by tensions in secondary education than difficulties in primary (Smithers and Robinson, 1992). Tensions still exist in the subject; the relative weighting on designing and making; balance of elements within the subject (i.e. construction materials, textiles, food); the place of assessment. To some extent, evolution in a subject as young as design and technology is inevitable, but it can produce a frustrating workload for primary coordinators who are teaching a class full-time, coordinating design and technology and possibly another subject or aspect of the curriculum.

Design and technology education is not the same as design and technology. This may sound confusing, but is important. There are many thousands of food technologists, constructors, householders and others who design and make in the real world. Children will design and make real things in the real world — as teachers we are educationalists, and need to focus on providing high quality design and technology **education**. This means providing coherent programmes of education which ensure progressive achievement for all within a broad and balanced curriculum. We must never forget that the primary context includes eight other subjects and where these relate positively to design and technology, we in primary education have a considerable advantage over secondary colleagues, for whom links with other subjects can be difficult to foster.

As was said earlier, we are teaching design and technology in primary education so that the next generation will be confident and able to see a place for technology in many areas of their lives. We may be able to encourage some children who will go on to study the subject in higher education and who may become designers or engineers.

Design and technology education encompasses a wide range of human experience that may be reflected in the primary context in the relative ease with which cross-curricular links are established. The following links are often made with design and technology:

with science	– materials, their characteristics, uses
	– electricity, its use, components, circuits
	– forces, how they affect structures
	– investigations, to test structures, materials
with mathematics	– measures
	– shape and space
	– scales
	– plans
with the arts	– design
	– form
	– dyeing
	– stitchcraft
	– theatre
music	– amplification
	– materials
	– insulation
English	– communication
	– modelling
	– planning
	– imaging
PE	– balance
	– sequences
	– movement
	– clothing
history	– housing
	– clothing
	– travel
	– theatre
	– medicine

All of the above present opportunities for design and technology education. They are very important as they provide contexts within which design and technology may be applied. Design and technology cannot take place in a vacuum (Kimbell et al., 1996). If one is designing or making something for the kitchen, it is important that you know what goes on in a kitchen. It will help you to know how kitchens have previously been designed and what tasks will be performed in the kitchen. Your designing and making will be furthered by talking to people who work in kitchens about their needs and it will help you if you understand some of the vocabulary of kitchens.

As well as researching and being knowledgable about the context and the needs of the users, the design and technology coordinator needs to be able to step back, to view the whole, to consider new ways of doing things, new approaches and new products. A great strength of primary education is the expertise primary teachers have in developing a theme or topic around which they will construct the curriculum over a period of time. Primary teachers are experienced at identifying and introducing contexts and ideas in ways which will be meaningful to the children. It is within such contexts that design and technology education will be most usefully placed, thus the child is immersed in a context where familiar and new ideas can be addressed. Vocabulary is familiar and yet will be developed. Design and technology becomes the vehicle for subjects like maths, English, art and science. Existing products can be examined and evaluated, improved or provide the basis for a new round of designing and making.

A useful definition of technological education was provided by the Association of Science Education which was part of their policy statement in 1991.

> *Technological education should form an integral component of the educational experience of all young people aged five to nineteen years. As a consequence of this experience and that obtained in other subject areas, students will be better prepared to develop an awareness and appreciation of the world, its cultures and the influence of the past, present and future technological change.*
>
> *Initially, young pupils should be encouraged, and helped to identify tasks in familiar contexts, which they are able to complete by drawing upon their present knowledge, understanding, experience and other skills. In doing this, and in following other tasks sensitively introduced by the teacher, students will develop and extend their technological capability until they become self-sufficient, independent of the teacher and able to identify 'needs and opportunities'. In time, they should have sufficient confidence to generate, evaluate and present their own designs and acquire higher order skills in order to fulfil a particular task. As a consequence of this progressive development in their technological activities and abilities, young people will be enabled*

FIG I.2
The design process

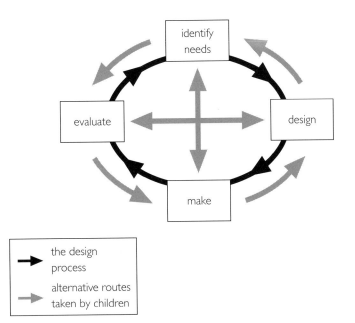

to play an active part in the control of their environment and encouraged to participate in its positive development for those less fortunate than themselves. The development of techno-logical literacy and capability will also provide many young people with relevant and appropriate preparation for adult life and employment. (ASE, 1991)

Design and technology has been defined in terms of 'the design process' (Williams, 1990). This process shows four stages or phases which a design technologist will utilise. The grey arrows on Figure I.2 recognise that young children rarely follow the simple model of the design process. They are more spontaneous and creative. The design process is most useful as a planning or review tool for the teacher. It is a framework against which the teacher can plan and review the experience of young children.

An alternative to the design process was a model proposed by Kimbell et al. (1991) where designing and making are seen as an iterative process (Figure I.3) as the hand and the mind interact, or 'to and fro'. The first model (Figure I.2) is perhaps the most straightforward of the two and is understood by many teachers as it was the basis of the earlier version of the National Curriculum for design and technology. One advantage

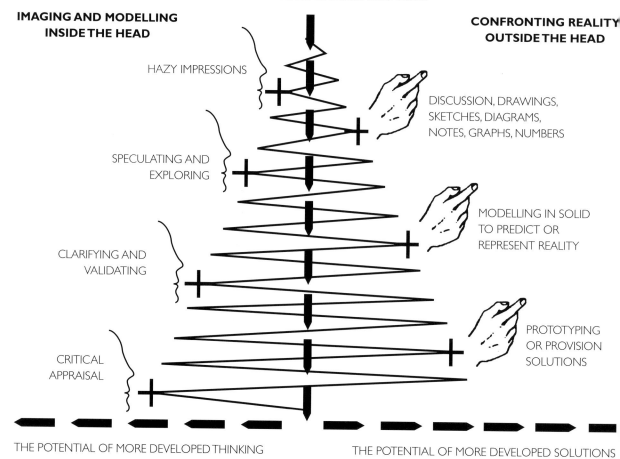

The interaction of mind and hand

IMAGING AND MODELLING INSIDE THE HEAD

CONFRONTING REALITY OUTSIDE THE HEAD

HAZY IMPRESSIONS

DISCUSSION, DRAWINGS, SKETCHES, DIAGRAMS, NOTES, GRAPHS, NUMBERS

SPECULATING AND EXPLORING

MODELLING IN SOLID TO PREDICT OR REPRESENT REALITY

CLARIFYING AND VALIDATING

PROTOTYPING OR PROVISION SOLUTIONS

CRITICAL APPRAISAL

THE POTENTIAL OF MORE DEVELOPED THINKING

THE POTENTIAL OF MORE DEVELOPED SOLUTIONS

FIG I.3
The APU model of interaction between hand and mind in design and technology

of Kimbell et al.'s model is that it implies use of the brain rather than merely what might appear to be passively following a flow chart. Significantly, these models assist us but are unable to capture fully the creative aspect of design and technology, that moment when the child images or imagines a new way of doing something.

Important considerations about design and technology

Kimbell et al. (1996) emphasise as do others, the importance of the user of the technological product, Kimbell et al. use the term **client**. Teachers and children should consider that while it may be fun or purposeful to make something they ought also to consider the extent to which it is fulfilling the need of the user or client. Simply identifying and talking about the user or client can be an important educational step in design and technology education.

There is a valuable tradition in primary schools of **model making** but a note of caution should be sounded, while the making of models is important alone it is not necessarily design and technology. There ought to be occasions when children make products which are full-sized and can be used i.e. a maths game, an art apron, a pencil stand, a healthy sandwich.

All design and technology comes from **human need**. In school there is some artificiality as the task almost always comes from the teacher, therefore, the type of tasks set, and how they are set, is very important to design and technology education. Tasks must be meaningful to the children and this is best achieved where the task comes, in some way, from the children themselves.

We should also draw children's attention towards **constraints**. Some constraints will be beyond the control of the teacher, i.e. space, range of materials. Teachers should, however, use constraints such as time, cost and so on, to add to the challenge and the learning potential of the task. By drawing the children's attention to them at the planning stage children can be more realistic in their plans.

All of the above necessitate a **practical** approach to this subject. Piaget (1929) drew attention to the active participation of the child in the learning process, which implies that children need to build from concrete experiences. The ability to think about abstract ideas begins for many children in their later infant years and continues throughout the junior years. The child is seen to make sense of their surroundings, organising ideas into schemata by the processes of assimilation and accommodation. Ritchie (1995) and Baynes (1992) provide separate and very useful summaries of learning theory and influences on young children's learning in design and technology.

One thing that you must do as an existing, new or aspiring coordinator for design and technology, is to refine your understanding of design and technology as part of primary education. Part 1 of this book asks the reader to examine those things which might be taken for granted about the role and to attempt to be clear in the role of coordinator for design and technology. This is an area that the coordinator should come back to during annual reviews of the subject in school. You might like to consider keeping an informal diary which will become a chronology of events in the subject, but which might also trace a changing view of the role by yourself.

In Part 2 attention is turned specifically to what the coordinator needs to know. There is emphasis on subject knowledge in design and technology and pedagogical knowledge in the teaching of design and technology. Both areas are a concern for design and technology coordinators. Most teachers are sufficiently intelligent to grasp technological concepts. The pedagogy is a little different, as it is more personal to the teacher. Aspects of pedagogy, like classroom management, often cause the teacher most cause for thought and attention. The final chapter in Part 2 is important, as it looks at the way teachers develop in design and technology and, in particular, how you as coordinator can assist them.

Part 3 includes a section on school policy for design and technology and follows the theme of 'practice into policy'. A policy document can be seen as the interface between what a school does and what a school says that it does. A policy cannot be a prediction about what might be, it is only useful if it tells us what is. Thus the policy must be flexible and able to adapt to reflect changes and developments in the school. The policy should be seen as responsive, supporting the view of this series of books that we should indeed put 'practice into policy'.

Part 4 of the book deals with the monitoring of children's achievements in design and technology and will consider first the larger scene of what we want to know and why. This section will then look at practical approaches for teacher, coordinators and senior managers in order that they can gather and use that information. There is an emphasis in the section on assessment on the role of the child in self assessing and recording which is based on an earlier work (Cross, 1994a).

Resources are always going to be important to the teaching of design and technology. It is essential that you make them available and manage them well as they are only a part of the fairly complex provision which needs to be made in a primary school for design and technology. The coordinator may wish to place considerable emphasis on resources early on, particularly if monies are made available. Comprehensive advice is given in Part 5 of this book, however, resourcing must be seen as a long term issue and should be balanced by equal emphasis on organisation of resources, of the curriculum and attention to how the subject is taught. Design and technology continues to develop as a subject in primary education. It was made compulsory from ages 5 to 14 in the UK in 1990 (DES, 1990a). The UK was the first country to make the subject compulsory across this age range (Layton, 1991). We have seen a rapid and continuing evolution of the subject. Curriculum coordinators in primary schools are in the vanguard in these developments. They are the people who will enthuse, reassure and promote the subject. All children will no doubt benefit, but girls may be the largest single group to gain greater access and reassurance in order that that they may contribute fully to a technological world.

This book

This book offers practical steps for primary design and technology coordinators. It recognises that this is one subject of nine in a National Curriculum which itself forms only part of what occurs in primary schools. The reality of the limitations of time for coordination and resources in a primary school are understood and the book attempts to offer purposeful approaches to the role in this context. Thus a design and technology coordinator will be encouraged to target action, to get things moving and to set achievable objectives for the role.

This series promotes the notion of 'Practice into Policy'. The policy of a school can only reflect what is going on in the school. The policy document should represent accurately what is happening in classrooms as a way of achieving the school's clear aspirations for design and technology.

Conclusion

An important final point relates to the need for a coordinator and leader in each school for design and technology. It relates to the priorities of primary education. Ask any primary teacher what is the most important thing in the curriculum and they will refer to some aspect of literacy, after which will come numeracy. This is as it should be. In almost any priority list design and technology is unlikely to be in the top group of subjects, this should be accepted, given the emphasis on literacy, numeracy and science. This is reason enough for design and technology to have a strong advocate in the design and technology coordinator.

As a coordinator for design and technology you are in a special position. As a somewhat new subject, teachers are going to require assistance and may be happy to admit that they need help. The children usually love the subject and whilst parents may not be as interested as they are in subjects like reading, they are usually in favour of their child having a technological education. Thus there are a number of positive forces around you to assist progress. The subject is large and needs to be approached methodically and with some enthusiasm. As we shall see in the first part of the book, your own view of the subject and your role in it is very important.

Part one

The role of the design and technology coordinator

Chapter 1

The role of design and technology coordinator

Introduction

The importance of this first step may not be obvious at this stage. We all have a view of what design and technology education is and what we want for young children. It is important that if you are going to raise children's attainment in design and technology, write policy in this area, lead colleagues and deal with visitors to the school, that you have thought through what you mean by design and technology. It is particularly important that you are quite clear in your own mind about the role of design and technology coordinator in your school. How you see yourself and how colleagues and others see you is very important and will influence the extent of the effect you can have on the design and technology in the curriculum.

Perceptions of the role

As coordinator of design and technology your perception of your role will be affected by:
- any design and technology (or related subject) which you were taught;
- other subject coordinators you have worked alongside;
- your reading (including the National Curriculum);
- your background knowledge;
- the extent of your personal training for the teaching of design and technology;
- teaching the subject;
- your colleagues;
- the reaction of children to the subject;
- the relation of the subject to others (e.g. is it valued in the same way as say, mathematics?).

As coordinator you should be aware of the multiple influences that are going to come to bear upon decisions, on you and on how others see you.

Your view of the subject will be very important. As the subject is new and evolving (Kimbell, 1995), you ought to be prepared to review your perception of design and technology education. We might ask whether it is possible to have a fixed view of technology in our modern world? New technology appears all the time. When Neil Armstong walked on the moon he did not have and had never seen a digital watch! Would we, during the 1980s, have predicted the growth in the use of mobile communications? New technology promises much in the future. An example is nanotechnology which promises machines so small that they will be released into the bloodstream of people and animals. Sensitive, for example to blood pressure, these tiny machines will automatically release drugs at prescribed times in exactly the right place within the body. There appears to be perpetual development in technology and as teachers we need to mirror at least some of this evolution and be prepared for further development in our view of the subject. As you begin to accept such ideas it may affect your understanding of design and technology, its teaching and the role of the subject leader or coordinator in the primary school.

How should a school make use of subject coordinators?

Your answer to this question will affect your perception of the role of the design and technology coordinator. If you and your school are going to invest valuable time and money in this role, you ought to be very clear about why you are adopting this system and what you hope to get out of it.

The days are gone when the subject coordinator (if the school had one) solely managed a cupboard containing tools and perhaps dealt with mail from relevant educational suppliers. The appearance of coordinators has resulted from two areas of pressure acting upon primary schools. First, pressure on headteachers, to manage resources, the budget and staffing and to monitor and evaluate every aspect of school life. Extra responsibilities for senior managers has led to a need to delegate work and in most cases responsibility. Deputy heads and senior teachers might have taken on these responsibilities but usually shoulder a considerable school management burden and (in primary schools) they often have a full teaching load, therefore the weight of responsibility is further delegated. Second, pressure also comes from the curriculum. As the nine subjects were introduced in the 1980s and 1990s as part of the National Curriculum, primary teachers began to collaborate in planning their whole school curricula in a way which had not previously been widely practised (Webb, 1993). Such collaboration requires leadership and as the National Curriculum is based on subjects there is logic (in many schools) in devising leadership roles based on the subjects. Exceptions include the many schools with a very small staff. Here subjects are sometimes grouped, while in other areas schools form clusters (Vulliamy and Webb, 1995). However, even in medium-sized primary schools (250–300 pupils) the number of curricular and other responsibilities usually outnumbers the staff so that teachers have to take responsibility for more than one subject or aspect of the curriculum. This immediately affects the reasonable expectations we might have of a teacher who also teaches a class full-time!

Primary schools and their teachers require leadership in all subjects. This is very much the case in design and technology as the subject is relatively new. Just a few years ago many primary schools did not have a coordinator for design and technology (HMI, 1992). It is a subject that offers a number of challenges, not least its practical nature. For the coordinator of design and technology these challenges present opportunities, as teachers are going to appreciate leadership. You will find that in the main, teachers are happy for you to provide leadership. And will need to have some system around them which can provide advice and guidance. The subject coordinator is perhaps the first and the most appropriate provider of support.

Leadership may be vital, but it is different from expertise; however, leadership is well informed by expertise. Leadership in this role can be seen in a range of tasks with which a curriculum coordinator should engage: write a policy, obtain and maintain resources etc. There is also a creative and inspirational element which is enabled by the ability of the coordinator to lift their head above the day to day business, see the way ahead, advocate, communicate, listen and lead colleagues towards a shared goal.

The subject of design and technology is generally seen as being based upon the 'design process' (see Figure I.2) (DES, 1990a) or other models (see Figure I.2 and writers like Layton, 1991). Development of design and technology education as a subject within the school will present needs for resources, training, documentation. The job of the coordinator is to identify, examine and, alongside colleagues, fulfil those needs. There is a strong case to argue that the subject benefits from a 'design and technology approach' to its coordination (Cross, 1994a). Curriculum design, curriculum planning, spending, organisation and teaching styles can each be directed to addressing those needs. There will be systems and even products to be fashioned by yourself and colleagues as you determine schemes, write and implement policy. As in children's design and technology, evaluation of this curriculum development is essential. It will be most important for you to evaluate the school's progress in the management and delivery of design and technology in your school. You will need to know what has to be done and you also need to know about the effects of your hard work.

Considering the nature of the role

Does your school call you a coordinator or a subject leader? The title may not matter much but within certain boundaries your role will be similar to other teachers in other schools who have a responsibility for design and technology education. Even before the so-called 'Three Wise Men' report of 1992 (Alexander et al., 1992) there was discussion about whether primary children would benefit from specialist teaching in some subjects. Design and technology is a contender for specialist teaching as it is one of the subjects in which primary teachers feel least confident (Wragg et al., 1989). There are examples of coordinators who have taken on some specialist teaching. One taught design and technology to four upper junior classes on two or three afternoons a week for a term. Another was freed from her class to rotate around classes and deliver design and technology, usually with the classteacher present. In the main, such arrangements appear to last for a year or two but eventually the schools observed reverted back to design and technology being taught by the classteacher. Specialist teaching of design and technology in primary education, therefore appears to have some things to offer some schools in some situations, particularly in the short term, but in present circumstances is often unachievable.

The role which we see increasingly is of a generalist-coordinator: one who is a general classteacher and who coordinates or manages the subject. This person is usually building up his/her subject background and pedagogic knowledge as quickly as is reasonably possible.

Whatever your role, you may feel that you can specialise to some extent — that you can assist colleagues, promote the subject and gain background knowledge. For this you need support and some training and it will be necessary to discuss this with your headteacher. The head may tell you what is expected of you, but this expectation is, if possible, best negotiated. Attention within any such negotiation should turn to how you will be supported in your role as design and technology coordinator. There needs to be a recognition that for reasons beyond our control, design and technology is, in most primary schools, behind other subjects in terms of the development of teaching in many classrooms.

Considering your role across the primary years

A major personal opportunity which is presented to any subject coordinator is that of advising, supporting, monitoring achievement and teaching across the whole primary phase. How will you do this if you have never taught a particular age range? You need to examine the matter carefully.

Aspects of the coordinator's role

children's achievement	– here you need to develop your understanding of what different age ranges might be capable of in design and technology;
teaching styles	– you need to be aware of a wide range of teaching options and that whilst an option might not suit you as a teacher, as long as it is within school policy and achieves good results it is acceptable;
advising	– build up your own background knowledge of design and technology and how it is taught as part of primary education;
	– here you may be able to give advice but constantly couched in terms of, 'this has worked in other situations', 'might it be evaluated?' 'tried?' You might see yourself and your colleagues as action researchers as you explore approaches together in the classroom. Your presence as a professional or critical friend should assist them.

The opportunity for you to observe and even contribute in teaching sessions with different age ranges should be sought. This may be easier for your colleagues and yourself if you avoid the stance of expert.

The role of a 'critical friend'

As a critical friend you and your colleagues will need to share mutual respect. You want to be sensitive yet honest, supportive yet rigorous. That is, if there is a problem you ought to be able to talk about it. You have to be willing to offer friendship, support and advice as far as you can. A key skill for you to be effective in this role is listening. It is almost always a good idea to admit that you don't have an answer when one is not obvious. There may be aspects of design and technology craft skills that you have not yet mastered that colleagues can assist you with.

Establishing the limits of your role

It will be important for you to decide to what extent you are a professional teacher/coordinator or a technician to assist with equipment needed by colleagues. There is every likelihood that your role will include both aspects. The role of coordination is a middle management role so you must decide on the emphasis you will give it. Examine Figure 1.1 below: your role is not likely to be clear cut, therefore you will need to assess your particular interests. Do these eight cells represent your understanding of the role? You ought to play to your strengths but recognise areas where you need to develop professionally.

FIG I.I
Aspects of the role of design and
technology coordinator

MANAGER	COORDINATOR	ADVISER/TRAINER
Do you have vision?	Do you communicate?	Can you listen?
Will you lead?	Can you organise?	Can you advise based upon
Can you deal with	Do you get things done?	good practice?
responsibility?		Can you lead colleagues
Can you judge quality?		through activities?
ADVOCATE	**ASPECTS OF THE**	SPECIALIST
Can you give a sense of	**ROLE OF**	Examine all your specialist
purpose and interest to the	**DESIGN AND**	knowledge and how it
subject?	**TECHNOLOGY**	relates to design and
	COORDINATOR	technology?
PROFESSIONAL	EDUCATIONALIST	TECHNICAL
FRIEND/MENTOR	AND TEACHER	SUPPORT
Do colleagues turn to you?	Do you value teaching as	To what extent can you
Can you empathise?	a skill?	support colleagues?
	Do you see the whole	
	picture?	

We have already said that technology is evolving and that
that affects the subject of design and technology too. It has
been suggested that you see the role as similar to the 'design
and make' process (see Figure I.2). As the role evolves it is
unlikely that the role of design and technology that you take
up will be the same as the one you will be fulfilling a few
years later.

A job description

You will need to be able to articulate the role for your own
benefit, for that of your colleagues and any interested visitors
to the school. You might write a job description under the
headings in Figure 1.1 above, but you should follow any
advice your school might have for you in this task. You may
be concerned that you state the particular things you can
reasonably be expected to do. Try to avoid the job description
being either very general or merely a list of tasks.

Some listing of specific responsibilities associated with the
role might be used in some schools and may be useful for
you to help define your role. Some schools have generic job
descriptions for classteachers and subject coordinators which
are adapted to suit each subject.

Job description for a design and technology coordinator

- Aim of the Responsibility

  To promote all children's achievement in design and technology through good practice reflected in the school policy. The role will focus on good management, planning, leadership, professional development, monitoring and evaluation of the teaching of and children's achievement in, design and technology.

- Management

  To maintain the focus on children's achievement in design and technology. To ensure that curriculum planning for design and technology is thorough and covers all aspects of the subject within the context of the school's overall curriculum plan. To provide clear documentation which will state policy clearly and concisely, giving clear advice. To ensure the best affordable resources including consumable and capital items.

- Leadership

  To give clear advice and maintain the focus on children's achievement. To establish and maintain a policy for design and technology which is a true reflection of classroom practice. To cater for teachers' differing needs for professional development in this area.

- Monitoring and Evaluation

  To use all means available to determine the extent to which practice is represented by written policy. To regularly determine whether policy in practice is achieving what is desired in design and technology teaching and children's achievement.

Responsibilities might include:

- developing and writing a policy;
- maintaining and managing resources;
- managing or providing INSET;
- reporting to governors;
- assisting colleagues with classroom design and technology;
- communicating with parents;
- ensuring that design and technology is represented in and promoted through other policy areas: i.e. Assessment Recording and Reporting (AR&R), special needs;
- ensuring that activities are carried out in a safe way;
- ensuring that design and technology is delivered in a cost effective way;
- monitoring and evaluating design and technology.

Challenges for design and technology coordinators

Teachers' background knowledge

Design and technology has much in common with other subjects. One thing which is perhaps particular to design and technology is the extent of the lack of teachers' background knowledge and confidence. The size and breadth of the subject are unique as is the need for particular resources and an emphasis on safety. Teachers need to be happy with practical work in the classroom, which may have an effect on classroom organisation and management. Perhaps the most challenging area for some teachers is the need to give children a certain amount of control of the activity. Thus it is often found that issues like classroom management and pupil control are at the heart of problems teachers have with the subject.

Equality of opportunity

Design and technology is truly a subject for everyone. As it is so practical, so concerned with people's needs, it can relate to each person. Because of bias and, for example, images in the media, many individuals feel that technology is not part of their lives. With some groups of children, access will be a major issue. Six areas have been identified (Cross, 1994b) which might interfere with children's access to the subject:

- **misunderstanding** by the teacher of either the subject or the children's capability;
- the choice of **context** might disapply either girls, boys or children from an ethnic minority group;
- the use of certain **materials**;
- presentation of **tasks** (boys found difficulty dealing with open-ended tasks (Kimbell et al., 1991));
- use of **language**;
- ignorance of or an inability to deal with a child's **specific needs** (sensory, motor, cognitive, emotional, behavioural).

The coordinator's role in relation to other staff

It is your job to manage and promote design and technology. Your role can be defined and written on paper, but also it will be defined on a day to day basis as you interact with colleagues. What will be your relationship as design and technology coordinator with:

the headteacher?	a professional dialogue involving regular updating, with opportunities sought to involve the head, the head should have a clear view of the overall school development plan as well as funding
other subject coordinators?	dialogue is needed here so that duplication is avoided and so that worthwhile cross-curricular links can be exploited
coordinators of special needs, AR&R etc?	all policy should make use of practical subjects like design and technology
children?	you need to maintain a strong interest in the achievement of children throughout the school
parents?	parents are important to the development of every subject, they need to know why design and technology is important to their child and how they can contribute.

Conclusion — is your notion of the role evolving?

Many design and technology coordinators have in the past found that their perception of the role changes with time as they grow into the role and as the school develops its design and technology. It may be that your original idea of the role was very much to do with resources. This will not go away but may need to be balanced against the need for emphasis on things like teaching style and planning.

Chapter 2

Establishing yourself in the role of design and technology coordinator

Introduction

Here we consider the steps that you might take in order to establish yourself in the role of design and technology coordinator. The following should be approached positively and turned to your advantage:

■ the role may be new in school;
■ the role may not have been filled for some time;
■ you may be quite new to design and technology;
■ design and technology may not be fully developed in the school;
■ you may be newly qualified or new to the school or both!

The questions about how you see the role will be important for you to consider and develop further. You now need to make a start.

Getting to know your subject

 I go on as many courses as possible, I'm feeling more confident but things keep changing, the training has done me good.

(Primary Design and Technology Coordinator, 1994)

 I don't bother going on technology courses now, I know what they're going to say, I've heard it all before!

(Primary Design and Technology Coordinator, 1995)

We might speculate on the reasons why these coordinators gave such contrasting views. It might be interesting to consider the possible effects on the teaching of design and technology in these schools of the attitude displayed in these remarks.

Coordinators of design and technology need to be skilled and knowledgable and have to engage actively in keeping abreast of a rapidly changing and developing subject. A simple way to become informed about the subject is to write to a range of suppliers and publishers (see the list in Appendix A) so that you have a collection of catalogues and samples, which are often supplied free of charge. Attending courses and local meetings and conferences will allow you to speak to publishers, advisers, teachers and researchers. Joining with other local design and technology coordinators, establishing a link with the design and technology department at the local high school/s and any feeder schools/nursery will extend your professional network. Building up a small collection of books on design and technology will assist you in giving advice to colleagues and will help to keep you abreast of developments in the subject. Joining or getting information from professional associations like The Design and Technology Association (DATA) (see Appendix A) provides a further important source of information.

Finding out about design and technology in your school

This can be done in several ways and might usefully be organised as an audit of the subject. You need to be clear about the scope of such a review or audit and you should be in negotiation with the head or a designated member of the senior management team to ensure that you go about this in a way that will fit in with normal school approaches.

Audit headings

The areas below might be those a coordinator would be interested in auditing:
- documentation;
- teacher confidence/knowledge;
- planning;

- teaching;
- learning;
- standards of achievement;
- resources;
- assessment.

Each of the suggestions is a whole-school issue, so for example, you may want to speak to the person who wrote the teaching and learning policy. Each can be audited as they relate to design and technology, by you, separately. To make the list more manageable you might want to break it down. Have a look at the audit proforma in Chapter 11 (Figure 11.3). You could deal with documentation and planning which fit together well, for example children's learning and standards of achievement.

Where can I get information about design and technology in school?

You need to establish those things which you will have access to and you may have to rely on informal access to classrooms and children's work. Many school staffs agree to provide planning to coordinators so that they can monitor the subject and provide resources and advice. You should seek to avoid emphasis on compulsion, rather this should be seen as part of the team work which is a mark of a well run school.

Negotiate with the headteacher and staff for access to and availability of:

- school documentation (anything which mentions design and technology);
- long term and medium term plans;
- schemes and short term plans;
- the full range of children's work;
- classrooms;
- other coordinators.

If you are not given access to, for example, planning, you may want to say that you feel that this will limit what you are able to do.

It is useful to examine all school documentation. Does other subject policy documentation mention design and technology? Make a note of what is stated and add any issues to your short or medium term plans, as well as talking to the coordinator concerned.

Gathering evidence

Your audit needs to take place in the short term, a few weeks should be enough. Try not to pry — you want to discover at this stage what is happening, rather than what is not happening. You should aim for as full a picture as possible and teachers will open up if they feel sure that you are interested in what they have done so far and are looking to help them. You may have to tie in the audit with assisting and helping as teachers may feel that it is peculiar if you remove your assistance hat entirely!

Analysing your audit evidence

Evidence you gather is likely to be in the form of notes made during and after conversations. It might also include inspection reports, school documentation, draft documents that colleagues may be developing, assessment results, records of meetings, records of courses attended, summaries of personal expertise and training needs and lists of resources available.

Sifting and analysing all of this could be too much to do at once. It might therefore be sensible to take the sub-headings of the audit one at a time. When you have the evidence try to organise it in a logical way, i.e. Key Stage 1 or 2, age group by age group, positive and negative responses, under major headings. This might assist you to see patterns in the evidence. Then determine the scope of the evidence:

- What are the extremes?
- Where are the most resources?
- Where are they most scarce?
- Consider frequency within the evidence?
- Is it all the teachers who are saying this?
- Is it the infant classroom?

Beware of dismissing a piece of evidence if it appears to be on its own and unusual, for example a teacher who wants to

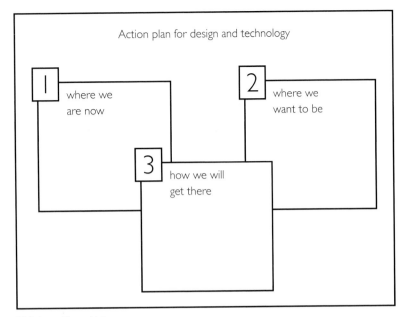

Figure 2.1: Action plan for design and technology — 1 where we are now; 2 where we want to be; 3 how we will get there

© Falmer Press Ltd

do design and technology in an unusual setting. Useful new ideas often appear for the first time in individual classrooms.

You might involve others in the analysis stage literally by asking them to assist you or talking the process through with someone. When you present your findings you will have to be wary of identifying individuals and use the presentation as another opportunity to gather information, perhaps through reactions to what you say.

It might be useful to present some kind of written or oral report. Keeping a diary or file will clarify your ideas, help you keep track of your work and give those who are interested access to a record of your achievements. A (short) written report is worthwhile as it is easy to make changes to it and gives the information in a more tangible form for the senior management of the school.

An action planning activity

Establish an action plan; Figure 2.1 will assist you in the first stages. You need to identify where the school is and where it

FIG 2.2
Examples of short, medium and long term objectives for design and technology

short term objectives (6 weeks–6 months)	medium term objectives (4–18 months)	long term objectives (1–3 years)
■ to discuss action plan with headteacher	■ begin to formulate the framework for a policy	■ consult staff on a draft policy statement and policy framework
■ to tidy the present resource	■ to hold a staff meeting at the resource ■ to construct a resource plan ■ to determine staff training needs	■ to organise resources so that they promote progression through the primary years
■ to audit present resources	■ to ensure a good supply of good quality construction tools	■ to ensure sufficient supplies of good quality materials and tools in construction, food and textiles

wants to go before you can make decisions about how to get there, therefore your audit acts as a piece of research leading to what is going on in school at present (see Figure 7.1, p. 95, for an action plan proforma and Chapter 8 for more advice on conducting an audit).

In the second box of Figure 2.1 you might include long and medium term goals. Short term goals might go into box 3 as steps along the road to the aims in box 2. If you are a full time classteacher and coordinator you must be very wary of the short and medium term plans — will you be able to achieve them? Try to ensure that the most important long term objectives are addressed in medium and short term plans at least in some way (Figure 2.2). At first plan for a termly review of the short and medium term plans based on progress. Remember that it is acceptable for your audit to tell you that you need to find out more about the teaching in an age range, for example. What you must do is build a plan of action to get that information.

These short, medium and long term plans are useful to organise and prioritise your work, not a stick to beat yourself with. If you are unable to achieve aims, reschedule them. If you seem to be achieving little, it might help you to seek advice from the head or other, more experienced members of staff who are, perhaps, coordinators themselves.

You should discuss your plans with colleagues including the senior management team who deal with the school development plan. Integration of your plans with the school development plan is essential and should assist you greatly in achieving your aims.

This action plan needs to be a short document which summarises where you are and what you are aiming to do in the short and longer term. Two or three short term objectives are enough at one time. It is better to set sensible goals and achieve them rather than set yourself unattainable targets which will cause you stress and frustration. Deadlines are important — you will inevitably miss some of them — but at least you will have some measure about how realistic it is to expect yourself to get things done.

Keeping colleagues informed

In the earliest stages you should discuss priorities with the whole staff. Do they agree with your analysis of the situation for design and technology? To a large extent their agenda is your agenda so you must be prepared to listen and take on board their concerns. The action plan will be updated and rewritten regularly. As a pattern of action becomes established you may find that a twice yearly review of your progress is sufficient. Dialogue with the head is very important and you should at least keep the head in touch with the latest version of the action plan. It would be sensible to get their sanction for any major changes which might affect the long term school development plan or which might require resources. It is also important to keep the staff involved by giving them opportunity to speak up on decisions you are considering. You should look for important areas where they can help to steer you. This consultation should occur with the whole staff from time to time, and also with individuals depending on their areas of responsibility and the age range that they teach.

Prioritisation

This will be important if there is a lot to do, which is highly likely in design and technology as it is such a wide and often underdeveloped subject. This does mean that you will have to choose which things to do first, balancing the desirable and the possible. It may be desirable to have children using a full range of materials, but it is unlikely that you will be able to achieve this in areas like food technology and textiles at the same time. Taking one at a time will give you a greater chance of success. Your colleagues will be able to assist you and will need to be involved in the decisions.

Successful coordinators may be those who can see the important things but can pace themselves so that things do happen. This might mean selecting things to do in the short term that are achievable, and taking the longer view for the bigger objectives.

Determining long, medium and short term goals

As was said above, you need to break up the objectives into achievable blocks. You might talk these choices through with colleagues, and including a member of the senior management team would be ideal. However, only you can be the judge of what you can do in the next six months. The hardest thing about this is putting off some very important things for a time, this can be a good idea as you need to associate your role with success and action. By pacing yourself you will still be there developing the design and technology in a year's time!

Documentation

Start by deciding what documentation is required and then put together a simple action plan, keeping everything as brief as possible.

One of the most important items to be dealt with early on is a list of resources. If you are going to do a stock take you may as well make the list available to the rest of the staff. This may be as simple as a list of contents fixed to a cupboard and might include the whereabouts of items. More advice about resources is given in Part 5.

Making your action plan public and allowing colleagues to steer at least some of your activity will give them some sense of involvement and you may even get offers of help! Publication of a proposed job description will further send out the message that you mean business.

Strategies

A diary

This does not have to be a day by day account of what you do, rather you would use it to record significant events. It might give you opportunity to reflect on developments as well as providing a useful chronology of events and developments which might assist you if you ever have to relate such developments to any colleagues.

MBWA (Management by Walking About)

Management by Walking About (Peters and Austin, 1986) was a popular phrase and approach in management circles a few years ago. It basically suggested that managers get themselves around and amongst the full range of colleagues on a regular basis. There may be a lesson here for coordinators. Primary schools are often geographically difficult places, in that classrooms can be on different floors or spread around a site and you could do worse as a coordinator than take a walk from time to time to see your colleagues after school. You ought not to make a nuisance of yourself, but express an interest in what is going on. It is worth looking at a range of work (within and beyond design and technology). You are likely to see a lot of design and technology in subjects like art, science, maths and history. A good knowledge of this and the work actually identified as design and technology will mean that you have a clear picture of the design and technology going on and how it fits into the whole curriculum. It will also assist you with colleagues who have a problem with the subject to identify aspects of the subject that they may already be doing.

Negotiate time in classes

This is most important because you cannot be expected to have a clear view of design and technology across the primary years if you have never seen each age range at work. Such time in other classes can be invaluable in monitoring the subject. The time slots can be brief, full lessons plus de-brief time is ideal, but twenty minutes slots can be enough to give you a flavour (beginnings and endings of lessons often tell you the most).

Focus on particular teachers

There will be members of staff more sympathetic to your ideas than others. It may be a good idea to encourage them and use them as a sounding board for ideas. New and young teachers may need support particularly and so by assisting them you may find that they are more willing to cooperate.

Buddy up

Establish an informal supportive relationship with another new coordinator. This will allow you to discuss things informally, provide each other with support and at least one member of staff with whom you have a positive professional relationship. Some schools make it part of school policy that each coordinator has an assistant or buddy. One significant advantage here is that if a teacher leaves, there is someone already in place to take over in the short term.

Making the role public

There will come a stage where you want to make people aware of your role and specifically the importance of the subject in the curriculum. There are ways of doing this which include holding staff meetings, issuing information, holding an exhibition, a parents' evening and open day or creating a newspaper. Such events will raise awareness amongst staff, children, parents and governors and may be used to raise the profile of the school locally and to involve people in the community. It will also put you in the position of having to hit deadlines, so be realistic, but this can help you to build up some momentum.

Drafting policy documentation

Policy documentation is dealt with fully in Part 4 of this book. Whilst its development is a fairly long term goal, you might look to make some progress on specific elements early on. The short statement of policy and list of resources available in school may be two good places to start. This will show colleagues and management that you mean business and will give them a clear indication of the quality and time scale you are working on. They may also learn to respect you as you are seen to be making progress.

Conclusion

Establishing the role of design and technology coordinator may be one of the most important things you achieve early on. It will be tied up with your personal credibility. Be reassured about this, you may not be the best teacher in the school but you can be a reasonable coordinator just by being organised. Any positive qualities you bring along (and we all have them) will be a bonus. Your recognition that you are part of a team will help you in many respects. A little genuine enthusiasm will go a long way to assisting your progress.

Chapter 3

Making the role effective

Introduction

This chapter may the most important in the book. It is possible to have many resources available in school, policies in place — and yet have unsatisfactory design and technology education. This is because there are so many other variables which affect the achievement of the children in design and technology. The teaching may be the most significant of these variables. The quality of the teaching will be affected by the quality of curriculum planning, assessment, monitoring and advice that is available for teachers, as well as the teacher's own expertise.

By teaching we mean all the behaviour that teachers exhibit that is directed towards children learning. See Alexander, 1992, for a useful discussion of primary pedagogy and what is meant by the term 'good practice', which includes things like organisation and also explaining, demonstrating and so on.

The effective design and technology coordinator:
- knows what is going on (monitors);
- can judge effectiveness of policy (evaluates);
- ensures effective whole-school planning;
- ensures that school policy is clear and reflects what is going on in school;

- emphasises – balance
                – progression
                – continuity
                – differentiation;
- ensures sufficient resource provision
- sees design and technology as part of a whole-school curriculum and the child's entitlement;
- acts to address training needs of staff;
- takes action following evaluation.

The words above are easy to state and yet difficult to deal with when you are a full-time classteacher. The last point about taking action is very important. If you organise yourself well you will spend considerable amounts of time gathering information and making judgments; this time is all wasted if it never results in change in policy or action of any kind.

Effective coordination should facilitate high achievement in the children. This emphasises the importance of monitoring and evaluation. After reading this chapter it is hoped that you will be convinced of the need for monitoring and evaluation of design and technology to inform you and your colleagues as the subject moves forward. As coordinator you can only be sure about the effectiveness of your role through careful monitoring and evaluation of the subject and your coordination of it.

A problem experienced by young teachers or those new to the role of coordinator is taking a view of the whole school. When you are a busy classteacher it is not surprising that your focus is mainly on the particular needs of the children within the four walls of your teaching area. Subject coordinators increasingly need to see the school as a unit. You need time out of your classroom to visit others in order to build a picture of the whole school. If such an opportunity does not exist you will have to visit classrooms outside the school hours. You will see children's work, either in their classrooms or on display around the school and be informed by looking at work the children do for other subjects.

Dialogue with the headteacher

The importance of the headteacher cannot be overemphasised. The head is likely to want to delegate both work and responsibility to you, but may be reluctant to lose touch. You may never know when the head will be approached by an outsider or when the head will see an opportunity for you or for design and technology. If they are well informed and have your role clear in their minds you are more likely to benefit from their action.

Never make too many assumptions about a headteacher's knowledge of your subject. They are often very articulate and knowledgable but may never have taught design and technology as part of the National Curriculum (by that name) — they certainly may not have taught it to all the age ranges. However, they have considerable experience, insight into the needs of the children in the school and an overview of the school and its staff.

Your dialogue with the head can continue in many ways both formally and informally. You ought to ask for an annual review of design and technology with the head or a member of the senior management team. You should find that headteachers and deputy headteachers are delighted to offer advice and help to you, particularly at the beginning but also on an ongoing basis where your work relates, for example, to the school development plan.

Regular reviews with the head or senior management staff ought to look at:

- children's achievement;
- your action plan and progress to date;
- your priorities;
- progress with regard to policy and documentation;
- any events which are planned;
- recent and future purchasing;
- your opportunity to monitor and evaluate;
- resourcing.

A short written summary from you made available prior to the review meeting will further discussion. Reviews with the teachers in school would also be desirable. Do they have a particular issue in mind? Do they see the improvements that have been made?

Keep the head informed, it is no good saying that you are short of equipment if you have not detailed the problem to the head! This should be complemented by informal communication. Show the headteacher high quality work from children, comment on the effectiveness of a new resource, mention good work going on around the school. Talk to the head about possible visits, outside links, parental activity. Try to balance the positive and the negative items you put to the head. Issues you present to them should be clearly stated and try to make sure there is some kind of resolution, don't expect the head to do it for you. Ensure that the head sees a fair share of issues resolved by you, as you want their moral and financial backup with the harder issues in the longer term. The head needs to know that time and money invested in you has a fair chance of producing some results!

Personal skills — relationships

You will establish a slightly different professional relationship with each of your colleagues. Communication is at the heart of the relationships. Frequency of communication may not be the most important factor — it may be that you communicate quite infrequently about design and technology — but that when you need to, you can. Your everyday professional relationship will be built on the numerous other encounters (non design and technology orientated) which occur either weekly or daily. It is important that you have a professional dialogue at some level with all colleagues and you may need to look for opportunities with your colleagues to set up a two-way dialogue. This may be away from design and technology at times, perhaps sharing a teaching resource, taking and giving advice, sharing a concern about a child or group of children or working together on some whole-school issue.

You need to remember that while it is your responsibility to take design and technology very seriously, it is unlikely to be as high on everyone else's priority list.

Where can you get help in developing your skills?

There are courses run for design and technology coordinators. However, these are limited in number and scope. Where they exist you ought to consider them very seriously. One important spin off is the professional network you will build up, including those who run the course and those attending the course. You ought to consider membership of a professional association like the Design and Technology Association (DATA).

Professional skills

Can you chair a meeting? Can you help a colleague to find the root of an issue in the classroom? Can you assess design and technology achievement in children? Do you have a knowledge of the books available in the school?

These are just a sample of the sort of questions you might ask yourself about your professional skills. They relate to your:
- own teaching;
- personal organisation;
- leadership;
- ability to support and advise.

You will be able to learn a lot from your own classroom and from those of your colleagues. You might consider a management or counselling course. There is little doubt that you will need to develop further your skills in listening, prioritising, time management, leadership and, of course, in the practical areas of teaching and managing.

Professional inversion

Beware, as an enthusiast for the subject you can easily step on the fragile ego of teachers who may have been at the school longer than you and who perceive you as a threat. The situation where younger members of staff perform better than older colleagues is called 'professional inversion'. It may be a fact of life, but you should work against the negative spin offs which will hinder your role. You need to ensure that all colleagues maintain their professional self esteem, while you are acting to improve their teaching.

Black holes

Some teachers, for whatever reason, may be rather negative towards you in your role. You lack the authority of the head so you have to fall back on your own credibility and the reasonable expectation that design and technology has to be taught. You can only seek to encourage, advise, clarify etc. You might, therefore, waste vast quantities of your precious time on someone who is experienced at resisting any pressure to change. Such teachers will draw all your energies and give back nothing — or worse — actively seek to undermine you!

You would be well advised to note, and even explore a little, the problem such an individual might have but to focus your efforts on more responsive colleagues. The school is likely to see better results flowing from your efforts and you are less likely to become downhearted. More often than not these 'blockers' or 'black holes' tend to come around when they see success going on around them. I have avoided suggesting that such individuals be ignored as they are important to the school. You may have to make your feelings clear to the headteacher though you might be well advised to keep these verbal and professional.

It is worth remembering that some teachers find teaching very challenging and practical subjects like design and technology can increase this challenge many fold.

Running up a down escalator

It has been said that school curriculum subjects never stay still. Children change, cohorts of children vary, teachers change, teachers vary and the curriculum changes. All of these factors appear to work against the coordinator. Therefore, it is said, if the coordinator stands still the downward escalator of these pressures take the subject downhill, hence you need to be moving forward all the time, even if it is a gentle development.

Parental involvement

This can be a powerful medium for development in the school. It is possible to have a range of positive effects by involving parents. Such involvement can include:
- parents assisting in classrooms;
- a design and technology newsletter or notice board (or section in a bigger one);
- parents' open days; and
- parents' evenings

Parental involvement is more than the sum of items like these. It has the potential to assist every aspect of the child's

A personal note

To what extent is it the coordinator's contribution that makes design and technology achievement rise? Obviously the classteachers need to take some of the credit. Subject coordination may be an area of professional work where we have to give selflessly and put aside personal desire for glory. The role is not macho, 'get out there an' sock it to them'; nor is it authoritarian, 'you must do it this way'. Good coordinators are advocates for their subject and work by stealth. You will be in a position where your personal strengths will be utilised to the full. Staying power is important, you are there for the long haul over several years. You will need to be able to listen, to turn problems into challenges, to show colleagues that where problems appear opportunities exist and to form good relationships.

education and can have a considerable effect on the lives of the parents and the school as a community. As a coordinator you will be aiming to have parents who: know about and value design and technology, know that their important contribution is valued and know that you have the responsibility for the subject.

How can you make yourself more effective?

You need to follow the advice in Chapter 1 and become increasingly clear about what you think is the purpose of design and technology and the role of the design and technology coordinator. You need to work on the:

- support you get from the headteacher;
- your management skills;
- recognition amongst colleagues of the role and your contribution;
- your background knowledge;
- your knowledge of children's learning in design and technology;
- your knowledge of where the school is up to in design and technology;
- your knowledge of how design and technology interacts with other subjects;
- your personal skills; and
- your professional skills.

There has so far been only fairly limited research in the area of primary design and technology education. Several of the books in the bibliography offer a reasonable picture of the present situation (see Kimbell et al., 1996; Ritchie, 1995). Whether or not you are ambitious you can use the role of coordinator for design and technology to help you develop professionally. It is an opportunity to show yourself and others that you can manage and lead.

Conclusion

This section and chapter encourages you to look at your role from the outside. To see yourself as design and technology coordinator as colleagues will see you. It suggests that you see yourself as part of the middle management of the school, this is the role of subject coordinators. Keep much of what has been said in Part 1 with you as you use ideas from the other sections of this book.

Teachers, coordinators and headteachers are often frustrated by the amount of paperwork and administration in school. There are aspects of this role which are administrative, but as you make a role for yourself as coordinator of design and technology do keep your focus on all the children and the excellent work that they do. Remember to follow the advice from Chapter 8 on assessment. You are interested in good and excellent work as that relates to what you would expect with children of this age and in relation to what that child has done before.

Part two

What design and technology coordinators need to know

Introduction

The importance of subject knowledge in design and technology for primary teachers has now been recognised (Ofsted, 1993, 1995, 1996). As design and technology is such a broad subject, gaining sufficient subject knowledge can be a daunting task: as a coordinator you will need to consider your own needs as well as those of your colleagues. Courses for primary teachers may be limited in availability and sometimes prohibitive because of cost, therefore, primary teachers and coordinators might usefully start from their personal knowledge base and build upon that.

In this chapter we try to provide a simple framework around which we might tackle important areas of subject knowledge. We must consider what a primary class teacher needs to know, as this affects what it is that a primary coordinator of design and technology ought to know.

One way to divide the knowledge required for this subject is to consider the process knowledge required and the background knowledge and understanding. As has been said earlier, design and technology is partly about choice. With knowledge the design technologist can make more effective decisions.

Subject knowledge in design and technology

Process knowledge

- designing
- creativity
- modelling
- context
- communication
- products
- quality
- prototypes

Background knowledge

In four areas:
- construction materials;
- graphics;
- textiles; and
- food.

Within each of these four areas there is a need for the teacher to have knowledge and understand about:
- materials available;
- manipulating the materials (cutting, folding, joining, etc.);
- tools;
- materials;
- components;
- electrical circuits, components or tools;
- safety (including hygiene in the case of food);
- mechanisms;
- structures;
- energy.

We will now look carefully at some examples from the lists above. This is to give you an idea about the breadth and depth which you should work on personally and with colleagues.

Examples of process knowledge

Communication
The importance of language must be stressed as design and technology education requires that the design technologist

(the child) understands a context or situation so it is essential that they explore a context which is familiar and meaningful to them. Exploration through discussion will be one very important way that children can begin to understand the 'problem' and thus to consider solutions. The language of orientation (above, below, inside, behind etc.) is a good example of a particular language which allows this kind of work to proceed. Words are often used, as in science, in particular or quite precise ways. Thus, when we use the word 'elastic' we may be talking about the property of any material to change its shape and then return to its original shape. A child referring to elastic is often speaking about an elastic band.

Design and technology uses other symbols for communication. These might include mathematical language, signs and symbols as well as scientific signs and symbols.

Children should be encouraged to communicate at every stage in design and technology. Design and technology will benefit and so will the children's literacy. A decision will have to be made about the best way to communicate: through mathematics symbols and language including graphs and charts; through scientific method; orally; in written form (if so which written form). There is also the question of the communication medium. Again we should be expecting the children to choose and to be able to justify their choice. Can they use electronic communication (telephone, fax, Email, computer, tape recorder)? Should they choose to write on paper, do they have choices here? If they are to use oral communication, to whom will they speak, for how long, will it be one-way or two-way communication? In what language or languages?

Modelling
Much primary design and technology involves children in model making. Sometimes the model is the finished item: a model bedroom containing model furniture and perhaps a lighting system. At other times, models (prototypes) are used to test out ideas, i.e. different designs for a food trolley (prototypes) for Mrs Wobble the Waitress (Ahlberg and Ahlberg, 1980). Elsewhere in this book it has been stated that children should, on occasion, produce the finished item, that

Each model maker has different things in mind: the child exploring a new idea or material, the architect wishing to communicate ideas to the client of the plane manufacturer ensuring that the plane will fly, be economic to run and be as quiet as possible. The householder designing a new bathroom. Models do not have to be three dimensional — scientists, mathematicians and design technologists can model on paper and in the mind with their ideas. Being able to create images in the mind and to manipulate them appears to be a characteristic of good designers. An example of a model is the design process (Figure I.2) mentioned earlier which to a limited extent helps teachers plan design and technology education.

is, a full size example of the product. Therefore teachers need to select options which will mean this is possible from time to time. Examples might include:

- items of clothing;
- desk tidy;
- bags;
- toys;
- maths games;
- lunch boxes.

These examples can be produced as full scale examples rather than scaled down models. They may include all the design features which the child has designed or a selection of them.

What we mean by a model appears to be a very simple question. There are differences and similarities between a model constructed by a child of four years, one constructed by architects designing a new store for a food retailer and a computer model of a new plane which allows aerodynamics to be tested on the computer screen. Obviously, each model is made for different reasons, some educational and others to do with learning about the design.

A model can be a three dimensional representation of an object, usually scaled down in size so that it is easier and cheaper to make, handle, evaluate and adapt. There is a limit to the accuracy with which a model can copy the full sized item, particularly in the primary classroom. Children and teachers in the early years will usually be delighted if a model copies reality in a number of respects; shape and colour, or a particular function such as an opening door. Older children and adults become more demanding and expect greater accuracy. This is an aspect of progression but ought to be approached realistically.

Children will often model spontaneously as they work through an activity. They will hold up components, try them in different positions and orientations. They are looking and imaging at the same time, trying to predict the consequences of one arrangement against another. This process would be well described by the iterative process in Figure I.3.

Teachers need to see modelling for what it is and make the most of it as a learning tool. Where children have made models as prototypes they are valuable as they tell the 'story' of the design process. Such prototype models should be included in display or reports about the designing phase.

How can children model?

On paper we can ask children to draw diagrams in order to 'model' ideas of what they intend to do. Children then benefit from the opportunity to talk about drawn designs. Construction kits provide a good medium for modelling as parts can be assembled quickly, ideas tried out, components moved etc. Children find it hard sometimes, to move from the kit to a material like wood as the two look different and have quite different characteristics. Modelling materials like Plasticine have been used to great effect where the child is designing shape or form. Such materials have little inherent strength and cannot include moving parts. Children might, therefore, need one modelling material to consider overall shape and another to consider a mechanism. They need time and space to model and it can be a solitary or group exercise. Children do benefit from talking their ideas through with one another.

Examples of subject knowledge

Manipulating the material

Children need to have time to explore and to be taught how to manipulate the new materials they come across as well as more familiar materials. What alternative ways exist to cut the material? Will some cutting devices be more suitable? In how many ways can this material be joined? Which methods are strongest? Which methods are waterproof? Can this material be scored? Will it fold? Does it have sharp edges?

Knowledge of materials is an important part of design and technology in primary education.

Components

Within the area of construction materials we are talking about the limitless number of items with which we might build or use to construct a model, i.e. wheels, axles, buzzers, lights, springs. A component is simply one part of a whole. In primary technology the design and technology coordinator ought to be aware of the components that are available in the school and the components that ought to be available to different age ranges of children.

> Primary educators are often forced to look for the cheapest components which are the most versatile. Plastic or paper straws are used widely. Versatile components are of particular value — examples include cardboard tubes, plastic 25 mm film canisters, plastic disposable syringes. It is worth talking to colleagues about the components they find the most useful and considering how you might introduce new ones.

The constraints of cost you will experience with materials in school are similar to the cost constraints experienced by 'real' designers in industry (children's technology is real!). For young children, so much is novel and new that even simple materials present a serious challenge. There is, however, a strong case that older juniors need to have available a more challenging and a wider range of materials (see progression in Chapter 6). Thus an annual budget is required to ensure the range of components necessary.

Safety

Of paramount importance to all teachers, safety often affects their approach to this subject. At the extremes are a small number of teachers who are so nervous at the prospect of children using tools that they avoid such activities. At the other extreme there may be some who through ignorance or lack of control allow children to do things that they should not. As coordinator, safety and teachers' knowledge of safety issues in design and technology are of paramount importance. You should be aware of advice about safety and hygiene (ASE, 1990; NAAIDT, 1992) and you should look for regular opportunities to update and refresh the knowledge of colleagues.

Safety should be dealt with separately in the school policy for design and technology. Children should be encouraged to take increased responsibility for safe working. It might be a section on a proforma: 'I will take care not to . . .' or 'Areas of danger include . . . I will keep myself and my friends safe by . . .'.

It is essential that teachers are able to show children safe ways of working and to allow children to consider the risks associated with the task.

Mechanisms

Teachers need to know the basic principles of levers, gear wheels, pulley wheels, axles, wheels, hinges, handles and catches. An obvious starting point is to look at the mechanisms around us, i.e. zips, bottle openers, doors, nuts and bolts and scissors. A good idea to develop is that of input and output. Mechanisms have moving parts, which pass movement through the mechanism. Movement energy is passed from an input through other moving parts to an output.

Example 1

Look at a can opener.

Question — What is the output of the can opener mechanism? i.e. what is the work that a can opener does?
(It may assist you to find and examine the operation of a can opener. Can you see which part of the tin opener pierces the metal lid of the can? How does the mechanism then continue with the cutting of the metal?)

Answer — It might be described as the initial and continued piercing of the can lid until the lid is cut off partially or entirely.

Question — What is the input on a can opener mechanism?

Answer — The turning of the handle.

Can you improve on the answers given?

Example 2

Look at a zip on an item of clothing.

Question — What is the input on a zip mechanism?

(It will assist you to examine the operation of a zip carefully.

Can you see the parts which push the two sides of the zip together? Can you see the individual teeth? Can you see the way that they interlock? Can you see how each tooth is designed to interlock?)

Answer — The pulling on the small tab or handle?

Question — What is the output of the zip mechanism?

Answer — The interlacing of the two sides of the zip which fastens the two halves together.

Try examining some other simple household mechanisms. What is the input/output on a stapler? a fountain pen? a food whisk? a shoe? It is important for the children to see how a mechanism works by looking carefully at the moving parts. How does each moving part affect the others? How is movement energy passed through the mechanism? When doing this with children it is probably essential that the significant parts are large and visible. You can extend the activity by moving to familiar mechanisms with either small or hidden parts — a computer mouse, a ballpoint pen, a clockwork toy, a tap.

Simple examples like those above are very useful and although we know them well can still be quite challenging. Think about the hinges of a door, are these a mechanism? Could this book be described as a mechanism? What are the moving parts? What about an umbrella? Can you identify all the moving parts and how movement energy is transferred through the mechanism?

Gears

It is advisable to get hold of a set of gears so that you can physically try the arrangements in Figures 4.1 and 4.2. A child's construction set which contains gear wheels will be very useful at this stage.

When two gear wheels have cog teeth which interlink and mesh, one will drive the other (see Figure 4.1). Where two gear wheels are meshed in this way and we turn one by hand we call this gear wheel the drive gear wheel. The other gear wheel which turns as a consequence is called the driven wheel. The drive gear wheel and the driven gear wheel will turn in opposite directions, one clockwise and the other anti-clockwise.

G 4.1
wo gear wheels interlinked

FIG 4.1
Two gear wheels interlinked

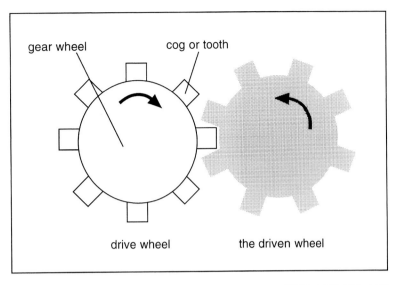

IG 4.2
A larger gear wheel drives a
maller one

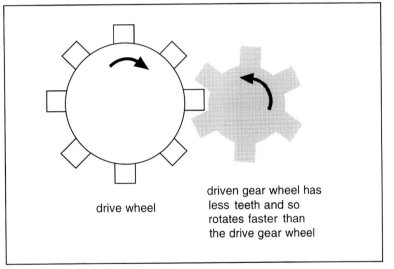

When two gear wheels are the same size and the cog teeth are interlocked they will rotate at the same speed but in opposite directions. Where these two gear wheels are different in size (see Figure 4.2) we will observe a difference in the speed of rotation in each of the wheels. Where the drive gear wheel is the larger of the two the driven wheel will rotate at a faster rate than the drive gear wheel. In the opposite case where the drive gear wheel is the smaller of the two we should find that the driven gear wheel (the larger) would rotate at a slower rate than the drive wheel. Thus we can achieve arrangements of gear wheels which will slow or increase the speed of rotation.

It is important for children to play with gears to see the meshing, realise that there is a drive and a driven gear wheel, see the change of direction and the change of speed. These appear to be important key concepts. As teachers we can seek to teach these and the associated language and hope that the children might apply them. We could move on from here to consider different types of gear wheels, perhaps idler gears, gear ratios etc.

Structures

Primary design and technology is often about making strong structures out of weak materials. Spend a few minutes looking around your home or thinking about structures in school. Examples might include: furniture, fittings, components of the lighting and heating systems as well as the building itself. You and the children are surrounded by a wide range of materials formed in different ways into structures. How many different kinds of chair can you find in school? Are the features of each chair wholly functional? Has the designer been creative? Is the chair built for an adult or a child?

As has been said, children should use a range of materials, some of which will be strong and rigid and others more flexible. A tent is a good example of a structure using a range of materials which are put together in a particular way to do a specific job.

Structures often derive their strength from stress within the structure. A cantilever bridge uses large beams which lie flat but are out of balance (see Figure 4.3). That is, as more mass within the beam is on one side of the fulcrum, the beam will support the load of traffic crossing the bridge without collapsing! Examples exist of bridges which were unable to stand the forces put upon them, for example the Scottish Tay Bridge Disaster, 31 December 1879 (Thomas, 1972).

Energy

In design and technology we often harness energy. Energy can be defined as the ability to do work. In this sense, 'work' refers to any task and thus has a wider meaning than the one we often use in everyday conversation.

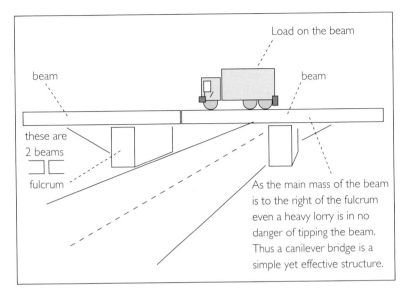

A clockwork alarm clock does the 'work' of time indication and of ringing pre-set alarms, a microwave cooker does the 'work' of heating materials, a computer does the 'work' of displaying and processing information, a windmill does the 'work' of grinding corn and a television does the 'work' of displaying pictures and making sound.

What 'work' would you say a car does? What 'work' does a torch do?

All the items mentioned above use energy. That energy comes in different forms. Which of the above use electricity as their source of energy? What other energy forms are used by the other examples? (chemical energy — petrol, food, wax etc; strain energy — a stretched spring or elastic band; energy of movement — wind energy, any object moving; heat energy; sound energy)

An important form of energy is one which we may call movement energy. This form of energy is all around us in things that are moving (cars, air, people, water etc). Scientists call it kinetic energy. Primary teachers must talk to children about the different forms of energy and not forget this one. Because we live on a large object (earth) which has a force of attraction towards its centre (gravity), movement energy appears to be lost as things slow down and stop, but the energy is not lost, rather it is converted into a new form. The problem for humans is that we cannot see it. A good example is to think of a car skidding to a halt. Where does the movement energy go? Some is converted to heat energy in the brakes, wheels

	input energy	'work'	output energy
wind-up toy	muscle energy (your arm muscles)	the toy moves	movement energy and a little noise energy
a motorcycle	chemical energy (petrol)	movement	movement energy, noise energy and heat energy

and road surface. Some is converted into sound energy. Energy cannot be destroyed but it does change its form. It may appear to disappear, but is never lost from the universe.

The wind-up toy gets its energy from the muscle in the arm that winds it. This energy of movement is converted to strain energy in a spring inside the toy which is released slowly through a mechanism which uses the energy to turn gear wheels and the wheels of the toy. Thus the energy is converted back into movement with small amounts of energy being converted into sound and even some into heat because of friction. Thus we can see an energy pathway:

movement   strain   movement   noise   heat

energy   >>>>> energy >>>>>   energy   + energy + energy

As children progress in science and technology they ought to begin to be able to identify different forms of energy and energy conversions.

In design and technology we often have to think carefully and try out prototypes to decide which form of energy to use, to see how energy will be used, perhaps in a vehicle, or look at the effects of energy in cooking, for example.

Tools

The advice given here is generic to any tool and is presented as answers to a series of questions which you might ask of any tool. To assist you the example of a wood saw is given.

How many types of the tool exist?

As design and technology coordinator you ought to be aware of several.

The basic saw used in primary education is the junior hacksaw which comes in a variety of shapes and sizes. Some junior hacksaws are very cheap, others allow easy removal and replacement of the blade. Some have different shapes of handles which mean that they might be more suitable for different children. Saws are rarely handed so you don't need to buy left-handed versions. Primary aged children are often introduced to the Gents saw, the Tenon saw and sometimes to the Coping saw and the Fret saw.

Children should come across the different types and designs so that they can choose between different saws. One way that you can show progression across the years is by allocating different saws as appropriate across the years.

Is the tool used in conjunction with other tools?

Use of any saw requires that the wood being cut is held still. An older child may be able to hold a piece of wood still on a bench hook (if taught the correct technique). Younger or other children may benefit from the use of a G clamp with the bench hook and others will prefer to use a vice.

Where children wish to cut accurately at 90°, 60°, 45° or 30° a mitre block is essential.

Younger children will require assistance or careful supervision when fixing wood in a vice, block or clamp prior to sawing.

What are the essential things to teach to a child?

Children need to know how to use the tools safely, how to pass the tool from one person to another, how and where to store the tool and a little about general care, including changing blades or bits (as appropriate to their age).

The junior hacksaw is a fairly safe tool in the hands of a sensible individual. It should always be picked up and held as in Figure 4.4. The wood to be cut should be held still in an appropriate device (bench hook, clamp or vice). The wood should be marked with a pencil to show where the cut will be made. The table should be protected. The child should stand when cutting and while holding the saw in either the right or left hand should apply pressure onto the wood with the other hand. This pressure should hold the wood still. The first cutting actions should be made in one direction only, towards the child, this should be done at least three times and will form a slot in which the child can proceed with a smooth to and fro cutting action. While sawing the child should try to use all of the blade, the blade should not be twisted, the child should keep their eyes on the sawing and the sawing should not be rushed. There is no need to press or rush as a sharp blade will cut, driven by the weight of the saw itself. It is useful to pause occasionally to check that all is going well and to take a short rest.

FIG 4.4
The correct grip for a junior
hacksaw

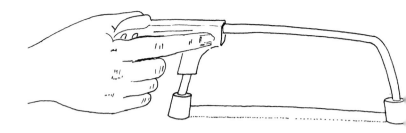

What are the safety issues?

Children need to know how to maintain a tidy workplace
and general safe practice with tools: never running, avoiding
walking around whilst holding a tool, never putting tools on
the floor. They need to know how to use tools safely; for
example, it is very important to know that with sharp blades
we need to work away from the person. (Always question the
need to use any blade which is so sharp; see Chapter 13 on
resources.) Tools need to be kept in the best possible condition
and should be the best quality you can afford. As coordinator
you need to be able to reassure colleagues that using the correct
techniques will make tools safe for their particular age range.

For what age range is this tool suitable?

Others may be able to offer advice, but you will also make your
own judgments by observing children using a range of tools.

What maintenance does this tool require?

A job can only be done well if the tool is in good condition.
No matter how skilled you are, if the tool is damaged or worn
you cannot expect first rate work and might, in extreme cases,
put yourself in danger. The tools recommended in this book
are proven for their reliability and safety. However, you should
ask does this tool require:

- servicing?
- sharpening?
- spare parts?
- cleaning regularly?

Children should be involved in caring for tools. All tools
need to be kept clean and to be visually checked regularly.
This may be more important for tools in food technology than
for needlecraft but similar principles apply.

How will we store this tool?

Tools should generally be stored in an orderly manner so that they are not damaged in storage and so that access and retrieval is straightforward. A wide range of storage options are available. Tool boards and trolleys offer neat, well organised and ready-made resources. Why not involve the children and turn yet another issue into a design and technology opportunity? Teachers need to ensure that access to tools at inappropriate times (e.g. playtime) is controlled. Some children may be able to act responsibly.

What is the cost of this tool?

Costs vary, but you should generally go for the best that you can afford, or at least middle of the market. You want tools that are soundly constructed, that will be easy to maintain and will last a number of years. You should obtain a range of catalogues to compare prices and quality, or buy from a local store where you can handle the tools prior to purchase. Many educational suppliers will gladly bring tools along to school for you to look at and handle, and will offer you advice. Encourage colleagues in the early years to avoid buying 'toy' tools, it is always better to use 'real' tools.

What quantities of this tool does the school need?

Here you need to talk to colleagues. You should be aware of the teaching methods teachers want to use or that are expressed in school policy. If class-teaching is going to dominate, for example, you might need sufficient tools to have one between two children to even one each. Where design and technology is taught in a group situation you might be able to contemplate smaller numbers. You also need to look at the curriculum plan for design and technology and perhaps other practical subjects. If you have three classes using needlecraft equipment at the same time it will cause a very high demand on equipment, but this can also be addressed by looking at the curriculum plan and adapting it to avoid such overlaps.

Where can I find this information?

A number of good resources exist which contain useful information. Covering the breadth of design and technology across the seven years of primary education plus nursery education is a challenge. The books and sources in Appendix A will assist you as coordinator in supporting colleagues.

Conclusion

Where colleagues have limited knowledge it may be very sensible to limit the scope of what each person teaches (at least in the early years of implementation) so that they can build up their knowledge with your backing. As design and technology coordinator you need to build your own background knowledge more quickly and more widely than most classteachers. You may not be an expert in all areas of design and technology, but you must make a start at building your knowledge and finding out where you can get that knowledge.

Chapter 5

Pedagogical knowledge

The central role of teaching

In the previous chapter some indication was given about those things which need to be taught in design and technology; this chapter focuses on how that teaching takes place. Design and technology should be taught to young children, however, this common sense statement belies a number of important questions. There is some evidence (Cross and Harrison, 1995) to say that for a number of years for a number of teachers, classroom design and technology has been based on children exploring and making with a limited range of materials and with little or no emphasis on teaching. What we need is a better understanding of what the word 'teaching' means in relation to design and technology. Good examples have always existed of teachers who are able to strike a balance in this subject between direct teaching and providing freedom for children to design and make (Makiya and Rogers, 1992). Design technologists have some freedom, but are usually limited by the constraints of time, cost and so on. It is the same in the classroom, materials and time for example, limit the things children can make. Teachers need to give children opportunities to design and make in an increasingly independent and creative way, at the same time teaching appropriate skills and understanding.

Most teachers have personal preferences and styles but need to recognise that some approaches work better than others. It is

OBSERVABLE PRACTICE	CONTENT	whole curriculum subject/areas		WHAT should children learn?
	CONTEXT	physical interpersonal		
	PEDAGOGY	teaching methods pupil organisation		HOW should children learn and teachers learn?
	MANAGEMENT	planning operation assessment of learning		
IDEAS VALUES BELIEFS	CHILDREN	development needs, learning		WHY should children be educated in this way? and WHAT is an educated person?
	SOCIETY	needs of society, needs of the individual,		
	KNOWLEDGE	children's way of knowing, culturally evolved ways of knowing		

FIG 5.1
Educational practice: a conceptual framework (Alexander, 1992)

unlikely that any one teacher has refined the most effective way of teaching any aspect of the curriculum for all children. There is emphasis in the next chapter on children's learning and the teacher's response, but because of the complexity of defining the word 'teaching', particularly in the area of design and technology, we will benefit from examining Alexander's (1992) framework (see Figure 5.1), which uses the term 'observable practice' to describe the behaviour we most commonly refer to as teaching. We will also use the notion of Alexander, Rose and Woodhead (1992) of 'fitness for purpose'.

What style of teaching best fits the children and the content to be dealt with? Alexander's (1992) framework (Figure 5.1) and his idea of pedagogy (teaching method and pupil organisation) and management of the classroom accounts for everything we might include within what he calls educational practice and encompasses what could be called in the widest sense 'teaching'. For most teachers in the primary years, Alexander's 'observable practice' is likely to relate closely to their own vision of teaching design and technology. The **content** of the subject, the **context** in which it occurs (already emphasised as most important), the **pedagogy** and **management**. Teaching styles or methods and management of the classroom are often confused one with the other. They are inextricably linked but can be considered separately. When discussion teaching methods we should avoid the sterile discussion of progressive methods versus traditional methods. You might seek to explore a mixture of approaches — a 'fitness for (the) purpose' of teaching design and technology.

Within educational practice Alexander also included ideas, values and beliefs which can easily be overlooked in busy schools. However, they are important for design and technology. As design and technology and its products are so much part of human activity and culture, its pedagogy must be informed by consideration of:

> **children**, their needs, learning and relation to the subject; **society**, what society needs and how individuals fit into society and how design and technology is part of that relationship; **knowledge**, how children know, what they know and how culture affects knowing.
>
> (See the work of Layton, 1992b and Siraj-Blatchford, 1993)

Having dealt with content, the focus now will be on the pedagogical aspects of teaching design and technology. The teaching of design and technology appears to involve the consideration of a number of tensions, important ones include the following:

- How does design and technology relate to other subjects?
- How should I manage it in the classroom?
- How do I ensure sufficient freedom to design and make while ensuring that I teach?

Teaching design and technology

After a series of recent interviews with design and technology coordinators the following list was constructed of behaviours associated with the teaching of design and technology: *demonstration; copying an existing model; questioning; directing; oral instruction; written instruction; modelling; intervening; explaining; discussion; identifying needs; discussing resources; visits; walks; examining existing products; children teaching each other; researching; teaching skills; making; planning; designing; using construction kits; drawing; play.* These behaviours are in no particular order, nor are we given information about the frequency of occurrence. This list is based on a small group of teachers and so cannot be truly representative, but it does give a picture of a breadth of teacher activity. The list of behaviours above might be usefully split into three categories:

strategies where the teacher is overtly teaching	demonstration, questioning, oral/written instruction, intervening
media and contexts which enable teaching and learning	play, construction kits, researching, examining products, visits, walks
activities promoted by the teacher where the child takes a degree of control	drawing, planning and designing, modelling

The first category includes activities where the teacher is overtly teaching by addressing, questioning or demonstrating to a group or class. The other two categories can be included in a broader definition of teaching and all the behaviours are characterised by the fact that they are controlled, planned and implemented by the teacher. Many of these strategies are used by non-teachers — doctors, shop assistants, farmers. What appears to characterise teachers is the combination of these activities, the style of their use and most importantly the objective. In teaching design and technology, teachers may use strategies they use in other subjects, however, their objectives should be specifically about children's progressive achievement in design and technology. Thus, clarity about objectives and knowledge of the children should guide the teacher in choosing teaching strategies.

Teaching a craft skill in design and technology

This may seem very obvious, but this important aspect of teaching design and technology has been identified by inspectors as being included in only a proportion of lessons (Ofsted, 1995). A child may need to learn a new skill for cutting with a drill.

Suggestion

Is it a good idea to experiment with class and group situations? A good strategy is to teach the main points to the whole class and follow this up with group work.

The child needs to learn how to:

- hold the drill;
- start drilling;
- place the bit in the drill;
- use a smooth action;
- avoid pressing down;
- clamp the wood they are drilling so that it does not move;
- avoid drilling into the tabletop below;
- how to remove the bit from the wood.

The teacher needs to decide based on knowledge:

- when to teach this skill;
- how different children might respond;
- how many children will be taught at a time;
- what are the key things the child needs to know/be able to do;
- whether verbal explanation, written explanation, practical demonstration, practical experience or several of these are required;
- what are the implications of this teaching for classroom organisation?
- what resources are required?
- how much time is required?
- how can this be presented in a stimulating manner?
- how to be sure about the extent to which children have learned the above?

Teaching a design skill

Developing design ideas

It is more difficult to provide teachers with advice here. The overall message may be more important than the detail. That is, designing is a skill and we can only develop that skill in a positive environment of design where ideas are respected and where outcomes are not determined from the start.

Children need to learn that:

- they must be clear about the objective — what will the user or client want from this product?
- putting yourself in the place of the user can help;
- in the early stages any idea is a good idea;
- sketching, imaging and talking with others can help;

- existing designs can be adapted;
- modelling often assists;
- unusual materials and components may assist.

The teacher needs to decide/know that:

■ children often lack confidence;	→ children seek help and reassurance
■ clarity about the purpose assists; by limiting resources too much we can severely limit the opportunity for designing;	→ using only paper and card can limit possibilities
■ that new contexts and materials can cause difficulty;	
■ careful teacher intervention can assist greatly;	→ 'Tell me why you chose to put the wheels on there?'
■ questions from the teacher can focus attention and challenge assumptions;	→ 'Do all lunch boxes open in in that way? Tell me about others you have seen?'
■ children need to practise sketching and imaging;	
■ discussion amongst children assists greatly;	
■ having to come up with more than one design often assists;	→ the children can evaluate each design and compare them
■ that the child is the best arbiter of quality as long as they are guided.	→ an important decision must always be made about the quality of workmanship the client expects

Examples of teaching approaches

Demonstration

This could easily be part of the examples above. Rather than using prolonged and complex verbal descriptions of how to carry out a task, teachers can provide a simple demonstration.

Sometimes this will be the teacher personally demonstrating, on other occasions this will involve asking a child to demonstrate a skill. Demonstration demands that those watching observe carefully, they need time to watch and to be attentive, they should be encouraged to ask questions. When a demonstration is occurring it is important that all those observing can see and are actively engaged in observing. The teacher must have good control of children's behaviour (avoid having children behind you) and ought to keep the demonstration as short as possible.

By asking children to demonstrate, the teacher avoids the impression, easily created, that only 'experts' can do this properly. It is a good personal experience for a young child to demonstrate a skill, giving an opportunity for some children to show their capability. It also allows those watching to consider problems they too might experience — such as having enough strength to tighten a vice, how to thread a needle. It allows the teacher to correct common mistakes, to emphasise safety issues and to observe (and control) the children watching. It is important that the demonstration is clear and gives the right messages.

A written instruction alone would not be used to teach the safe use of a tool. Demonstration itself is not enough. Teachers need to move the children fairly promptly by putting their observation and the advice given into practice.

A useful way to reinforce the message might be to ask them to produce a poster — 'the safe way to use . . .'.

Try to ensure that for at least the first minutes of practice, and intermittently after that, you observe the children to ensure that they are following your instructions. After the effort of the demonstration the first minutes of children's activity are crucial.

Direction versus support

This is an important consideration for teachers of primary design and technology. The extent to which you as teacher should support and direct children will vary according to the age of the children, the task you are setting, their previous experience and their individual capabilities. Kimbell et al.

(1996) observed a number of lessons at Key Stages 1–4, judging the level of support and direction during five minute segments of lessons. Overall, they found that at Key Stages 1 and 2 there was a fair balance of support and direction. They found, however, that at Key Stage 3 the proportion of direction increased by several fold.

This balance that primary teachers appear to be achieving might be further used to affect children's learning. It may be that teachers need to decide positively how much they will support and direct in order to achieve particular learning objectives.

Intervening

All teaching may be considered to be an intervention. By intervention most of us mean a positive move, either physically or more often with words in the form of a question, an explanation, a word of encouragement etc. When considering how and when to intervene the teacher needs to be clear about:

- what the session is about (what are the expected learning outcomes);
- how the session will be introduced and concluded;
- planned intervention;
- unplanned intervention.

The most significant intervention is often the introduction from the teacher at the beginning of the lesson. Like the conclusion, this intervention is often planned. Often interventions during the lesson can be planned, perhaps a break after ten minutes to check that everyone is on task and understands the task, or an intervention after twenty minutes of designing just prior to the point when a class or group are about to start making. Interventions such as these may be used to reinforce particular teaching points, to assess, to encourage or to ensure safe working. They can be planned and unplanned. There will be times when the teacher observes children's behaviour or speech which indicates that some teacher assistance is required. This highlights the importance of teacher observation in a subject like design and technology. The teacher needs to be regularly observing the children and their work to determine the extent of children's progress. The notion of setting the children off and leaving them to it ought not to have a place in day to day teaching of design and technology.

We should consider the extent that our intervention is to support or direct. This is significant in design and technology as the subject is partly about children finding their own solutions and evaluating them. We are not looking to intervention as a device to constantly 'correct' children. Your intervention might be aimed at:

■ assessing achievement;
■ preventing frustration;
■ extending achievement;

and might be achieved by:

■ challenging the child;
■ affecting the direction of the child's efforts;

through:

■ questioning;
■ reminding the child about the purpose of the task or a teaching point;
■ examining an existing artefact;
■ looking at their own work very carefully;
■ focusing attention.

You might intervene with an individual, a small or large group or indeed the whole class. Many teachers have an intuitive feeling that individual intervention or teaching is the best approach. Because of the size of classes it is hard to see how it can be an efficient format for all occasions. Whole class and group intervention make much better use of the teacher's time. Before intervening it is worth pausing for a moment, as children often redirect themselves. While you pause, reconsider the intervention, could you give them another minute or two to see if the intervention is really needed? Is this something that the whole group needs to know?

How can you verbalise your concern?
Tell me where you are up to?
What is your next step?
Why have you .... ?
Tell me why you chose .... ?

Such questions are important as it is likely that despite your careful observation, you are not aware of their reasons for doing what they are doing, or what they are about to do. Their response may tell you that your intervention is not required. If there is still a concern, focus in with more questions so that you are able to guide or assist with minimal effect on their sense of ownership of the task.

Classroom management for design and technology

For all coordinators of design and technology this is an important area. For many teachers the subject of design and technology is a challenge: the subject knowledge presents one series of challenges, but the organisation of practical activities in the classroom may be far more significant.

In design and technology children need time and space as well as resources. Advice and issues raised here are provided to cover schools where classteaching predominates and others where forms of integration are used. This book seeks to avoid emphasising any one approach. It tries to point out advantages, disadvantages and things to look out for in promoting children's design and technology.

Space for design and technology
Repeatedly inspectors (HMI, 1993; Ofsted, 1995) have recognised that many primary classrooms and schools lack the space for design and technology. The subject of space will be referred to in Part 5 under resources, but we examine it here as it is so important to the teaching of the subject.

Where design and technology is conducted as a whole class, space may be restricted considerably. Children need desk or table top space for the times they are using construction and other materials to make things. They will need such space, too, when they are researching and designing. If children are to examine existing products and artefacts they will need a sizeable area to set things out, examine them and take them apart. Floor space is important for both older and younger children, although traditionally it is younger children who are given access to the floor. Many times a table top or desk is too small or unsafe and children will spread material, build models and trial them on the classroom floor.

It is worth considering the location of areas for design and technology work. Close to or in a thoroughfare may mean danger to the children who are working and to those passing by. Light is also important, the area should be well illuminated. Proximity to the teacher is important as the teacher needs to be able to work with others in the class and still have this activity in line of sight. Proximity of resources should be considered, as it is good to get children to select their own tools and materials.

Design and technology being carried out by individuals or a group can be quite distracting for other children in the room so it is worth considering whether it is possible to create any kind of barrier between groups. Plants on a table, drapes, children's work hanging from the ceiling can all create a feeling of separateness and even help to deaden noise a little.

Position of resources

Resources for design and technology need to be easily available. The coordinator needs to be aware of what resources are available in school and what should be bought if funds are made available. Where there is need, the design and technology coordinator should include them within the action plan or development plan for the subject.

Resources should be examined separately for each phase of primary education, each age range (see notes on progression in Chapter 13) and each class. They should be clearly labelled and kept as close as possible to any area where design and technology group work goes on. Storage of the resources is important and may require considerable expenditure and the collection of suitable containers. Trolleys of different sizes and purposes can assist greatly in some circumstances. For a fuller discussion of resources see Chapters 13 and 14.

Classroom environment and ethos

This should be one of a busy workshop where children and adults work together in a positive environment where everyone's contribution is valued and where there is much discussion and celebration of children's success.

Kimbell, et al. (1996) suggest three types of tasks in a hierarchy. These are:
- contextual tasks (very open);
- framed tasks (some constraints);
- specific tasks (tightly defined).

Considering the tasks to be set

As can be seen in Figure 5.2, design and technology tasks need to be considered carefully and might be short term (building block) or long term, more open-ended tasks. The number, timing and time available need to be considered. Advice might be included in your school policy.

FIG 5.2
Curriculum tasks which involve designing and making can be viewed as contributing to a spiral (Sheffield, 1991)

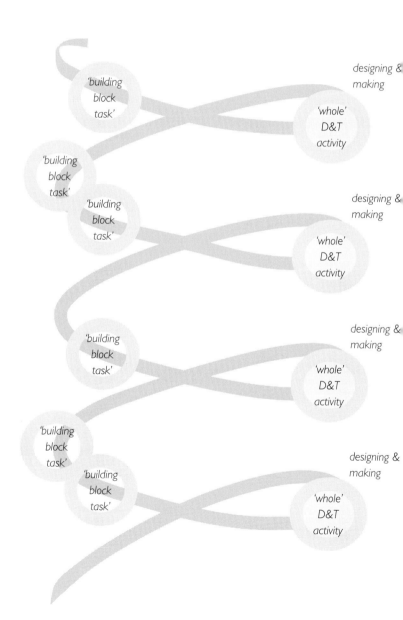

Kimbell et al.'s (1991) earlier work suggests that the task chosen is itself a very powerful determinant of children's achievement.

> *Tasks can be described on a sliding scale of open-ness and closed-ness . . . . . . the tighter the tasks become with proportionally less room for the pupils to negotiate them for themselves and develop a sense of ownership. Generally, the more open the task . . . . . . the better the girls perform. Much tighter definition . . . . . . appears to favour the boys.* (p. 208)

> *One is led to the somewhat sinister conclusion that it would be possible — given an understanding of the nature of these effects — to design activities deliberately to favour any particular nominated group or sub-group. More positively, it would also appear to be possible to design activities that largely eliminate bias or at least balance one sort of bias with another.* (section 15)

The Programme of Study for design and technology (DfE, 1995) refers to a range of categories of tasks which ought to be included in your medium and short term plans for teaching. These are referred to as follows.

Pupils should be given opportunities to develop their design and technology capability through:
1 assignments in which they design and make products;
2 focused practical tasks in which they develop and practise particular skills and knowledge;
3 activities in which they investigate, disassemble and evaluate simple products.

(DfE, 1995)

In Part 3 there is an example of a school's scheme where the topic plan for design and technology gives advice about when these would occur. The first category of design and make tasks (DMTs) represent a significant objective of design and technology. That is, children are put in a position where they design and make products. These products and the contexts from which they are drawn would become progressively more challenging. DMTs would be increasingly open-ended, with opportunity for the child to make more choices and more informed choices about products. Such tasks are very time consuming if children are going to have the opportunity to consider needs, designs, make plans, make the product and evaluate it. This means that such tasks might only occur perhaps three or four times in a school year. The amount of time devoted to these will vary but it might be as much as a third of the allocation in a term.

The focused practical task (FPTs) was included by the writers of the programme of study to encourage teachers to see a place for teaching, learning and practise of skills in design and technology. Thus a focused practical task might be one where a new tool, technique, material or aspect of knowledge and understanding is taught. These focused practical tasks might be shorter than DMTs and might be seen by most teachers as a lesson or half a day. It is likely that these tasks would be more numerous than the other two categories of task whilst the overall time devoted to them may be about equal.

The third category of task where children investigate, disassemble and evaluate simple products (IDE tasks) importantly focuses children's attention on the made world and the countless manufactured products around them. Thus, if children are going to design and make toys they might look at existing toys. If they were going to learn about gears they might look at gear mechanisms in kitchen whisks, hand drills, toys etc. and carefully examine them:

- can they identify the moving parts?
- can they accurately describe the movement of one of those parts?
- what makes it move? another part? a motor? a person?
- can they see and describe the inside of the product, i.e. a toy?
- if they can't see the inside, can they speculate about what is inside?
- can they close their eyes and listen to the product? what noises does it make as it operates?
- is the product strong? how could we describe the strength of a textile? and how is that different from the strength of a particular tower?
- what is the input? (what is the input of energy?)
- what is the output? (what work does the product do?)

A note of warning about the term 'disassemble'. The spirit of these tasks is that children examine the parts and functions of the parts of products. Taking things apart has a place in this work but it is likely to result in problems putting things back together. Try looking for scrap products that can be disassembled and later thrown away, try asking children to make working models in construction kits and then swop the model so that another child can describe it.

These IDEs will be fewer in number and might themselves be quite short. They are an opportunity for exploration and learning, important aspects of the Programme of Study and associated language can be delivered through these tasks.

All of the tasks above can be conducted by children alone, in pairs or in groups. Cooperative and collaborative capability is often an overall aim of a school. Design and technology is a subject where the opportunity to practise these social skills may often arise. Teachers should provide opportunities each year for children to work collaboratively and independently in design and technology.

The progression of these tasks during a term or half-term can vary, here are some examples where the termly time allocation of twelve hours is being used during a half-term.

PUPPETS — Year 2

	week 1		week 2		week 3		week 4 & 5
learning objective	**IDE** 1 hour	**FPT** 1 hour simple stitching	**FPT** 1 hour clarify design ideas	**FPT** 1 hour cutting & joining textiles	**FPT** 1 hour joining dowelling strips	**prep for DMT** 1 hour develop and communicate design ideas	**DMT** 6 hours (2 × half day) plan making process and make puppet/s
activity	looking at existing puppets	making finger puppets	designing a spoon puppet	making spoon puppet	make a spoon puppet with arms	design puppets for Charlotte's Web (White, 1952)	plan making make puppet/s

WEAVING — Year 5				
	week 1		week 2		week 3

	FPT	**FPT**	**IDE**	**FPT**	**DMT**
learning objective	2 hours introduce weaving incl. vocab.	2 hours create a design with warm colours	2 hours examine shuttle & heddle on real looms	2 hours construct and use a mechanism, examine control of movement	4 hours consider characteristics and properties of the textiles; determine how well made is the product; consider the effectiveness of the product
activity	card and peg loom weaving	box weaving	visit local textiles exhibition	in pairs construct box loom with shuttle and	design and make a wall hanging for the nursery with four colours to be used as a teaching aid heddle

Use of media which enables the teaching of design and technology

We referred earlier to play, construction kits, making and visits. Here we refer to the media or the medium chosen by the teacher within which the teaching and learning take place. The media is very important to a practical subject like design and technology. Thus nursery children require certain attributes from a construction kit (size, visual impact, ease of connection, familiarity, lack of sharp or small items). Older children can use kits with smaller more technical parts, colour remains important. Parts must fit together easily, older children can cope with more complex joining systems but may require the same high quality instruction and assistance necessary with younger ones. When considering the type of wood or boxes we might make available to children we need to consider the attributes of the media and its suitability.

Selection of context

Another series of important choices for the teacher is the selection of meaningful contexts for the children. The notion of moving from the known to the unknown is very useful here. Children respond well to contexts they understand: the school, the playground; the park; the doctor's surgery. Here they have visual clues and a vocabulary with which they are familiar. They are familiar with the needs of the clients in these scenarios. Another set of useful contexts are available in children's fiction, the Three Billy Goats Gruff (traditional), Incy Wincy Spider (traditional), The BFG (Dahl, 1982) are characters which appeal to different age ranges and with whom the children can empathise. This way a teacher can avoid unfamiliar contexts to start off and perhaps later begin to explore less familiar contexts as the children grow in confidence.

Teacher initiated activities towards independent learning

This will vary according to the maturity and the capability of the children in this area. As design and technology coordinator you may find that some teachers are very reluctant to move control of activities towards the children. This is often related to their level of confidence with the subject of design and technology or to issues of discipline. Early in their design and technology education young children will require short tasks which focus on one thing at a time. Teachers will need to identify opportunities in all activities for the children to make some decisions about: the materials; who to work with; the time available; when the job is finished. Later on this must be built upon as the children move towards open-ended tasks which require further independence. This is an opportunity for differentiation. If there are children with behaviour problems they may require very close supervision. There will be others, however, for whom more freedom will be appropriate.

Peer tutoring

There is a strong case for children supporting one another, particularly in a subject like design and technology. The teacher can use time efficiently by training a group or pair of children highly so that they are in a position to train others or provide a first level of support for others. Teachers often use this technique when dealing with computers.

Grouping

Whether children work individually, in pairs or in groups, has a powerful influence on what they learn from a task. Products made are often better for the input of a number of people. The factors which normally affect teachers' choice of grouping include: the task; the objective; the personal characteristics of the children; the time available; the children's ability to cooperate; friendship amongst the children. There are advantages and disadvantages with groupwork — but design and technology has a lot to offer those who want children to work together. As tasks become more complex forms of groupwork become necessary in order that several jobs can occur at the same time, as can be seen in the chart below.

	advantages	disadvantages
individual work	each child produces a product each child's work is obvious	reduced chance for collaboration teacher input has to be repeated
paired working	requires collaboration requires communication half the number of teacher inputs required?	some opportunity for one child to rely on the other or for one to dominate
small groupwork	opportunity for more collaboration opportunity for a team approach a need for cooperative planning teacher input is to the whole group when necessary can establish particular groups: i.e. all female	considerable chance for a child to 'opt' out demands a lot of the children

> One teacher who sought to establish groups of three asked each child in the class to write their name on a piece of paper and the names of two other children that they felt they could work with. The teacher then took away the slips of paper and constructed groups based on these choices. Most children were accommodated in a trio which included at least one of their choices.

This strategy could be adapted by asking for children to nominate three others, including perhaps one boy and one girl.

Adult assistance

Some teachers find the practical activity associated with design and technology very demanding. Although not normally essential, it can be helpful to have an extra adult available. As coordinator you might be able to suggest some assistance from an adult helper at least in the short term involving parents who offer to help in school. If it will assist a teacher to make a start or make an effort to improve things this is likely to be very worthwhile. However, we need to avoid any suggestion that extra adult assistance is essential as you are unlikely to be able to provide it.

There is an argument which says that if a teacher is having problems, that you as design and technology coordinator should be the one to assist. If the extra adult is a qualified teacher it may be possible for this person to take the class and leave the teacher with a group or to take your class so that you might give some classroom support. Another good alternative is a little team teaching where you work alongside the teacher.

Emphasising progression

Progression in children's achievement is perhaps the reason we have schools. It is essential that we are clear about where we want children to go in design and technology. Teachers are often pleased to have a school policy or scheme of work providing guidance as to what to include and when (see Chapters 8 and 9).

Assessment

This is dealt with fully in Chapter 11. The emphasis is on using assessment as part of the teaching process to inform future teaching. There is considerable potential for the child to play a role in assessment in design and technology as it can be seen as part of the design process. It does involve the teacher in paying attention to the children as they are working and to the children's two dimensional and three dimensional work.

Differentiation

This is dealt with more fully in the next chapter but is related to assessment. If children are going to get maximum benefit from the hard work the teacher is putting into planning and preparation then it is important that the plans take account of where the children are up to. This assumes some knowledge of what the children have done recently and some assessment of what this means.

Differentiation by outcome is often overlooked, but will remain very important in design and technology where children often tackle a similar task and respond to it at different levels. The task itself can of course be amended, simply asking the children to build a bridge with a span of only 6cms changes the task very significantly from one where the span is 50cms.

The degree of support given by adults is very important to children in design and technology. Teachers are normally seeking to make the children more self-reliant, which might mean working with other children rather than being led by a teacher.

How much design and technology?
The dilemma is that we want the children to become more independent in design and technology and yet we want to teach them skills, about materials, mechanisms and tools. The children will discover many things about design and technology for themselves, but not everything. Firstly, we need to establish learning objectives or outcomes that teachers can pursue, thus a whole-school curriculum plan for design and technology will assist teachers with statutory requirements (Programme of Study) and any other content or emphasis required by the school. Teachers then need guidance about how much design and technology they should teach as a proportion of the whole curriculum. Some schools have carefully followed the advice of the Dearing (1993) report, others have considered this advice and made their own policy. Others stipulate the number of topics and projects, some more prescriptively than others. All schools aim to ensure adequate coverage and balance. Campbell (1994) notes wide fluctuation from school to school and between governmental and school expectation and what actually happens in classrooms. The Dearing report suggested that over a 36 week school year the time allocation for design and technology for 5–6 year olds should be 36 hours (4 per cent of

time available) and for 7–11 year olds 45 hours (5.3 per cent of time available). This could mean an hour a week for the younger children and a little more for older ones. Most primary schools have opted to focus time during the year on specific themes, topics or projects, so we might find significant design and technology occurring on three occasions in the year and that such activity is quite intense.

Conclusion

Consideration of the issues in this chapter are very important in terms of teaching the subject. We can hope that as the years go by we may be in a better position to articulate what we mean by teaching design and technology. Perhaps the best advice to you as you develop in the role of design and technology coordinator is to maintain a constant dialogue with yourself about your own teaching and that of your colleagues regarding the subject. Keeping the teaching of design and technology under review is likely to remain and even increase as an important part of the role of subject leader. Remember that the only purpose of teaching is the progressive achievement in children's design and technology: this is the only criteria for good teaching.

Chapter 6

Children's learning in design and technology

Introduction

Research is somewhat limited in the area of children's learning in design and technology. This is particularly the case in the primary years, so while advice can be given, primary teachers and primary design and technology coordinators should see themselves as classroom action researchers. It is highly likely in such a new subject with new materials and resources that you will develop quite new classroom approaches which are wholly acceptable.

The reason that teachers need to know about children's learning in design and technology is that this knowledge can assist the teacher in making decisions which can be directed at furthering individual progressive achievement, progression being Alexander et al.'s (1992) 'touchstone' of education.

Why do we teach the subject — design and technology? How do children learn design and technology? These are questions which at least someone in each primary school ought to be able to answer. You might feel that it would be important for the school policy for design and technology to say something here. A design and technology coordinator needs an understanding of children's learning as applied to the subject as this will guide a range of decisions and will affect values. What is more important? The product or the process? Is a child's product educationally valuable if it bears no resemblance to their early designs?

Sources

We can draw on the educational theorists who have stressed the importance of practical activity, the active participation of the child (Piaget, 1929; Vygotsky, 1962), and who have sought to take account of that which the child already knows (Ausubel, 1968). There is much in writing about young children in science (Driver, 1983; Harlen, 1985) which will give useful clues as to how learning occurs in design and technology. The small amount of research in this area is useful as are your own observations in the classroom. Piaget saw the child moving through a series of stages from the simple biological mechanisms at birth to highly developed systems of abstract operations. Piaget, however, gave little importance to context and social setting. Donaldson (1978) and others repeated many of Piaget's experiments and showed that with a little thought regarding the meaning of the task to the child and the setting, children would be able, for example, to decentre. This is interesting for design and technology coordinators as context appears to be so important to children's work in the subject.

In recent years there has been recognition in the teaching of science that children bring along to any experience their own personal constructs about the world. This movement is often referred to as 'constructivism'. Constructivists suggest that the teacher's first step is to discover where the child is up to now and then seek to challenge those ideas which the child holds which run counter to accepted scientific views. We are often reminded that famous scientists (Galileo, Copernicus, Darwin) held views which in their lifetimes ran counter to the prevailing scientific view. This is not to suggest that all children's naïve views are right, but that we should keep in mind that present scientific and technological knowledge is a product of the past and is likely to be improved upon in the future. It is also worth remembering that design and technologists do not always need to know **how** something works, rather they need to know **that** it works and in what circumstances it might stop working!

Harlen (1992) gives a number of illustrations of children dealing with new observations. She describes how learners use previous experience to understand and explain the new

FIG 6.1

A representation of new phenomena and the formation and testing of new ideas (from Harlen, 1992)

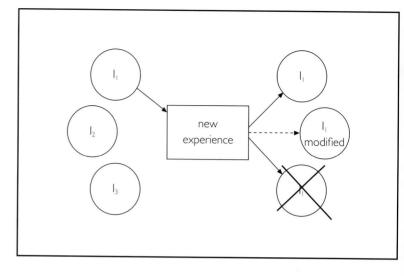

phenomena. She describes a group of children who explained the fact that newly varnished blocks of wood stick together by suggesting that the wood becomes magnetic when wet. We can think of other situations where a child might examine for example a fossil for the first time and might refer to it as a shell. Infants playing with floating and sinking objects were asked why the floaters floated and the non-floaters sank. One child suggested that it was because all of the floating objects were yellow as indeed they happened to be on this occasion!

Harlen uses diagrams like the one above to show how a

> number of existing ideas (I) which exist in the mind to be called upon to help understand the new experience. It may be that perceived familiarities between a previous experience and the new one results in one or more of these ideas being linked in an attempt at understanding. Other processes also may create links — for example communication, since similar words used in description may suggest connections. It is not always logical reasoning and careful observation which leads to ideas being linked, but creativity and imagination have a part. . . .
> . . . But once an existing idea has been linked its usefulness in really *explaining the new experience has to be tested.*

Thus some ideas are modified and others are rejected. Harlen made two interesting points as caveats which will be appreciated by most primary teachers. The first is that children's testing of ideas may be quite unsophisticated and therefore may lead to the wrong or erroneous conclusions, and second, that as children's experience is less than that of adults they will have fewer existing ideas to help explain new phenomena. This is bound to lead to children adapting ideas from a limited repertoire when those ideas are quite inappropriate. The teacher's role is affected by these, in that children's capability in testing (process capability) needs to be developed and teachers need to suggest new ideas which might be testable to determine fruitful areas of development. There is significance here for design and technology as children may be willing to try almost any combination of materials. The teacher needs to ensure that opportunities for learning are used, e.g. when a model built with water soluble glue collapses when wet.

Teachers' views of learning are very important to design and technology, a constructivist view sees the child 'starting' with a conceptual structure which by learning is progressively restructured. McGuigan and Schilling (1997) provide a number of examples of how teachers can 'elicit' children's understandings. Such a child-orientated approach does not see design and technology as a tap to be switched on and the child a vessel to be filled (with the teacher adjusting the flow according to the vessel's neck width!). Constructivism seeks to determine where the child is up to. Consequently it puts assessment in the correct place (see Chapter 11) as the tool which informs the teacher about the child's personal ideas, pointing the way so that subsequent lessons are well matched. The idea of match was advocated by Harlen et al. (1997 and 1992, p. 18). Match is a challenging notion, the teacher seeks to challenge the child so that learning occurs but to avoid the negative affects of failure which can demotivate.

Differentiation

More recently this aspect of match has been covered by the term 'differentiation'. Naylor and Keogh (1997) compare the views of Lewis (1992, p. 24) who sees differentiation as a process directed at individuals 'the process of adjusting teaching to meet the learning needs of individual children' and Ofsted who refer to groups: 'the matching of work to the differing capabilities of individuals or groups of pupils in order to extend learning'. They go on to offer practical approaches to differentiation, recognising that as teachers are human it is impossible to cater constantly for the individual needs of all children. It is important for coordinators to have a clear view of what they mean by differentiation as some teachers can react badly to a demand that they must differentiate in design and technology. You might usefully refer to Dewhurst's (1996) forms of differentiation, with differentiation by outcome being valued. Primary coordinators being primary teachers themselves will be only too aware that specialists often make claims for their subject which cannot be met realistically within the present primary classteacher system.

There are different kinds of differentiation, the five headings below are suggested by Dewhurst (1996).

differentiation by:	explanation	design and technology example
outcome	children all carry out the same task, children perform differently	all children construct a river crossing for the Three Billy Goats Gruff
task	different tasks according to different needs	able children are asked to make more than one suggestion
support	deliberately unequal investment of time by adult/s	extra support to a group of girls who appear to have little confidence
classroom organisation	e.g. ability grouping	putting quiet children together so that they have more opportunity to take the lead
resources	e.g. computer, special resource-based activities	a range of holding devices and saws to assist children with poor coordination

When teachers talk about differentiation, they often focus only on task differentiation which is potentially the most challenging form in terms of planning and preparation. Classteachers must be encouraged to use all five forms of differentiation above. There are ways to use task differentiation in design and technology with minimal addition to preparation. For example we might ask all the children to design a new kitchen apron. Some children in the class might be asked to consider one criteria i.e. strength. Another group might be asked to consider several — cost of production, water resistance, ease of use. This way the same activity can be made more challenging for higher achieving children. You see that such examples fall fairly naturally into Dewhurst's groups.

variable	Dewhurst's groups
■ number of properties to consider	task
■ the length of the task	task
■ the group selected to work together	classroom organisation
■ the detail of your instructions	support
■ whether the children are familiar with the context	task
■ choice of tools	resources
■ choice of materials	resources

By using Dewhurst's groups and/or these variables, teachers can tailor design and technology tasks to suit different children.

There is an argument which says that every now and then, at least once a year, children should be given a very open-ended task which will allow them to achieve to their best and thus give you a clear view of how they can achieve. Such a task would allow differentiation by outcome. If the advice in the last chapter about tasks is followed we ought to see these more than once a year in design and technology.

Progression

The reason that we might seek to teach well and to use different forms of differentiation is that we want children to progress. This book gives you advice in a number of areas on how progression might be achieved. Teachers need to be well informed about children and well informed about the subject.

Progression can appear in a number of forms:
- making choices about work, materials and tools;
- working in less familiar contexts;
- tasks becoming longer;
- using more techniques;
- working as part of a team;
- working more accurately;
- vocabulary;
- using criteria in evaluation.

FIG 6.2
Possible progression in the generic skill of cutting (based on Cross, 1994)

- tearing
- separating, dividing
- cutting pastry, plasticine
- cutting out pictures and shapes
- using sandpaper
- sawing activity
- using different scissors
- cutting along lines
- using a file
- using saws safely
- scoring
- making choices about cutting tool
- cutting paper with a rotary trimmer
- introduction to new cutting tools, i.e. junior hacksaw
- increasing accuracy
- establish criteria for the selection of a cutting tool, i.e. cutting around corners, speed, finish

In an earlier publication (Cross, 1994a), attention was given to basic or generic skills — skills which are needed in several aspects of design and technology and in other subjects. One such skill is cutting. Human beings require skill and knowledge about cutting different materials and about the tools that they might use. Primary teachers are used to teaching young children to cut with different tools; scissors, dessert knives, pastry cutters, hole punches, sandpaper. Primary teachers understand the steps associated with learning to use a pair of scissors. For design and technology we need to extend the range of tools (junior hacksaw, pinking shears, drill, rotary cutter etc.) and the children's associated knowledge. Then, when they are faced with a textile or plastic the children will be able to suggest which tools are most likely to be suitable. As design and technology coordinator you may find it useful to discuss this with teachers. Such skills are areas with which they will feel familiar and have relevant experience.

Progression in the generic skill of cutting (while some of these occur before others, there is a limit to the extent to which this can be seen as a hierarchy or strict progressive pathway) is shown in Figure 6.2.

Another generic skill would be joining. How many different ways can we join card, wood, paper, plastic? Children need knowledge and experience of adhesives, tapes, clips and ties etc. so that they can consider and choose alternatives.

These may be emphasised in your policy as progression, a key point of which is choice. That is, when faced with a situation, are the children developing a repertoire of skills and a body of knowledge to draw upon? One school decided to make the process skills in design and technology the emphasis at Key Stage 1 and quality of the product an emphasis at Key Stage 2. To assist colleagues you might build clear elements of progression into the scheme of work for design and technology using planning proformas like those in Figures 9.2 and 9.3, informed by advice like that in Figure 9.1. Specific advice about progression in skills is given in Cross, 1994a.

Conclusion

Design and technology might be a 'forgiving' subject here for both teacher and child because in open-ended problem solving situations there is rarely a single answer which can be called the right one. Design technologists designing a new garden wheelbarrow might have to weigh up the various uses; carrying heavy or bulky items against cost and even size, so that purchasers can carry the product away from the shop! With choices about materials, shape and weight different designers may come up with quite different but still 'correct' solutions. Perhaps the most important thing in design and technology education is the increasing extent to which the child as designer and maker can justify decisions taken.

Chapter 7

Helping teachers develop — your most important task

Introduction

In order to develop design and technology education you need to be informed about the subject in school. As coordinator of design and technology you ought to have accurate information about the expertise of colleagues in the subject. Do any colleagues have relevant qualifications? What about their experience inside and outside education? Before you can take meaningful action you need to be informed.

Your action plan should reflect your priorities for design and technology and you will need to ensure that these plans are reflected in the school development plan. Have a good look again at Figure 2.1 (Chapter 2) and its three questions which can be used as an approach to action planning.

Question one, where are we now? must be dealt with, hence you need to build up information about the needs of staff. Despite involving considerable effort, its answer requires only a description of what is occurring now. An audit (see Figure 8.3), which should be part of your approach to monitoring and evaluating design and technology, would achieve much of this. You need to find out about:

■ what design and technology is going on?
■ what is the scope of design and technology at present? (is all of the programme of study covered?);

Design and technology coordinator   **An action plan**

possible areas for concern

conduct an audit

areas identified

prioritise these

long term objectives

short term objectives

action to be taken   deadlines

review/evaluation when?   by whom?   success criteria?

IG 7.I

proforma for an action plan

■ how well prepared do colleagues feel to teach design and technology?

■ what standards of work are occurring (Where is the best work? Are there classes in school where there appears to be no evidence? It would be wise to talk to the headteacher or senior management team about this question);

■ when does design and technology occur?

■ what resources exist/are used?

Helping teachers to develop

This is an important aspect of the role of coordinators of primary design and technology. Teachers are likely to welcome constructive practical advice. Many primary teachers feel under pressure — for many, design and technology is an extra subject which has appeared recently. It is worth remembering that primary children are expected to take eight years to reach a particular level by the time they are eleven years old. Therefore it may be optimistic to suggest that teachers would pick up all they need to know about teaching design and technology in a short period.

Any general audit of the subject ought to consider the personal professional needs of teachers. This may focus its attention on subject knowledge but ought to address pedagogical issues as well (Chapter 6). Why not give a photocopy of part or all of the Programme of Study and a highlighter pen to each teacher and ask them to highlight the areas where they feel they need to develop their personal knowledge. Do they feel happy about food technology? construction? textiles technology? The priority must be ensuring that teachers know enough to teach what is required.

Design and technology tends to divide up into sections of background knowledge, i.e. construction, mechanisms, food, materials, energy and textiles. Each of these could be a focus for professional development, so that in your action plan for the subject you might take these on one by one.

A multifaceted approach may be the best way — with workshops, books, other resources, classroom support, CD

ROMs — providing different ways for teachers to gain in understanding, knowledge and confidence.

An audit of staff strengths

It may be better to lay some emphasis on the strengths of colleagues rather than looking only for weaknesses. You could conduct this simply as a questionnaire or as a series of informal discussions. The latter, whilst time consuming, may reveal more. The former will provide you with evidence on paper which may be useful to present to senior colleagues. Beware of those teachers who might use it as an opportunity to get negative messages across. What you want to know is which are the strongest overall areas for staff and which are the weakest and which directly affect teaching and learning.

Ensuring that you have an accurate picture

It is easy to assume that teachers know more about design and technology than they do. The audit and general discussion may reveal a quite alarming lack of confidence, but remember that the honesty and frankness of colleagues will be affected by their perception of you, your role and your purpose. An initial awareness raising session may allow everyone to look at the subject and share their thoughts.

Influencing and assisting colleagues

You and your colleagues are in a learning situation and it is part of your job to promote teachers' learning about design and technology. This implies that you might organise your colleagues' learning or even teach them. Depending on your experience and confidence you may or may not feel comfortable training your colleagues, however, there a number of approaches, some of which involve you in directly training your colleagues. Others are less direct.

Displays
You can use displays around the school to demonstrate good practice in design and technology teaching. When displaying

children's work add labels which explain the process, the designing and the making. A display might emphasise the range of materials used, the fact that youngsters worked individually or in groups, that safety was important. We all know that teachers look at each other's displays (usually for ideas). Why not harness that natural process to spread the word? Emphasise important words in your display — model, prototype, client, constraint, skills or mechanisms.

Classroom support

This can come in different forms. It might be as simple as offering advice about planning or classroom management. It can involve team teaching where you teach design and technology together or where the classteacher focuses on the design and technology and another teacher takes other children in the class. Involvement of another teacher, including yourself, should be used to best effect with careful planning and review.

Media

When colleagues are choosing television or radio programmes encourage them to look for ones which involve designing and making, problem solving and materials. You might record good ones and make them available. A number of companies market good quality pre-recorded video material.

Information Technology offers a good deal to design and technology through Computer Aided Design (CAD) packages, multimedia and communication (wordprocessors, Internet). Speak to the school's IT coordinator about using the design and technology and IT budget together to obtain some of these resources (see Chapter 13 and Appendix A).

Are there times when computers are not used in classes? Could a computer be made available in the staffroom with good, suitable software available?

Books

Teachers are usually very effective users of all kinds of books. They also value books and reading highly. Take a broader view of books as a design and technology coordinator so that all books in school can be viewed as potential starting points.

You ought to start a staff library for design and technology, perhaps investing in all or part of a published scheme. Talk to the teacher responsible for the school library, can you be consulted next time there is money to spend on the library? Could a design and technology section be formed in the children's library? Take a good look at the school's approach to reading. Is a scheme used? Are there sets of readers available? Could you base design and technology around a book that children use to learn to read?

> The Battle of Bubble and Squeak *(Pearce, 1978)* — *Designing play equipment for pets?*
>   Burglar Bill *(Ahlberg and Ahlberg, 1977)* — *Designing security for the house to stop Burglar Bill?* Charlotte's Web *(White, E.B., 1952)* — *Designing and making a new pig pen?*

Staff meetings

Can be directed at any of the above and might usefully look at individual aspects of the subject. Why not hold the meeting around a design and technology cupboard or trolley? Several companies who sell equipment will provide a salesperson to come along to school to demonstrate equipment.

It is likely that at some point you will need to organise a series of staff meetings. This might be three or four over a half-term or term, or a series over a longer period. Issues like planning and policy will have to be discussed and finalised at staff meetings. Basic awareness raising may be the place to start with a series of sessions, then addressing issues identified earlier. You may need to focus particular training and support at teachers who may be the only ones dealing with a particular topic such as computer control. (For general advice about organising and running staff meetings see Cross and Cross, 1994.)

Outside courses

Where these are available use them strategically to increase your knowledge and pass it on or ensure that colleagues get the opportunity to attend the course themselves. Outside speakers will often run day courses or staff meetings in school and these can represent very good value for money, with the whole staff gaining directly.

Conclusion — step by step

As design and technology is such a big subject, schools have found it difficult to develop several aspects at the same time:

- the design process;
- construction materials;
- food technology;
- textiles technology.

As you set yourself objectives, think in terms of breaking down the total task of implementation into blocks — you might have a major input on the first two above, followed by another on the second two. The extent to which you can deal with the breadth of the subject will be affected by:

- the school's present position;
- the time you have as coordinator;
- other priorities in school;
- availability of resources and expertise;
- funding availability.

Better to pace the development of the subject realistically and fall a little short of that than attempt to do too much, fall far short, or even worse, make mistakes. Ensure that you are well informed and that you are implementing a plan of action which is addressing and reviewing the issues.

Part three

Whole school policies and schemes of work

Chapter 8
Designing and making a policy for design and technology

Chapter 9
Designing and maintaining a scheme of work for design and technology

Chapter 10
More than maintaining

Designing and making a policy for design and technology

Introduction

In stating that it is promoting 'practice into policy' this series makes it clear that the dusty, dated and unused policy document sitting on the headteacher's bookshelf is a thing of the past. It is essential that the design and technology policy reflects what is going on in classrooms. There will, however, always be some tension between what occurs in classrooms and the accuracy with which the policy reflects this. At the interface between the two we find the design and technology coordinator promoting children's achievement in design and technology and informed by careful monitoring of that achievement. In fact it is the action plan devised by the coordinator which acts as the interface. The policy document should be responsive to changes and can be seen as a working document. As such it might be considered as being constantly under review.

The policy for design and technology must tie into the school development plan, both should be familiar to all the staff and be regular working documents for the senior and middle management in the school. The design and technology coordinator will need to be in a position to negotiate on behalf of the subject for time and resources with the senior management team. In such negotiation the design and technology coordinator can use a well constructed policy to good effect.

The start is an audit, leading to an action plan and hence action should include the writing of a structure for a draft policy based on staff consultation and discussion. This book suggests that your action plan is itself part of a process of designing and making the policy.

While you will get advice from books about what you should put into a policy for design and technology your policy must reflect what is going on in school. You will, therefore, have aspirations for the policy which will be reflected in your action plan but which can only be included in the policy after exploration, agreement with your colleagues and implementation.

If policy is developmental, 'evolving' from practice, the documents themselves will always be developing. You might want to call them 'draft' documents in the first year or so. You would be well advised to word process them so that changes can be made easily following further review.

This chapter assumes that the design and technology policy reflects and integrates other school policy in areas like teaching and learning, assessment, recording and reporting, special needs and equal opportunities. In order to do this comprehensively such integration should be supported and advocated by the senior management team. However, you can do a lot yourself for design and technology.

What is the purpose of a school policy?

The school policy and scheme of work should do a number of things. It should:
- clearly state what you mean by design and technology;
- emphasise the practical nature of the subject;
- detail long term plans;
- set out the ways in which progression in achievement is achieved;
- give teachers clear advice on classroom issues like safety, teaching, classroom organisation, assessment, special needs.

Schools should develop a distinctive set of policies. Different schools use the term 'policy' to mean different things. Here we will refer to three elements which in some schools are separate documents, these are; a policy statement, a policy document and a scheme of work. These can easily be incorporated into one booklet or a file. Such a booklet or file might also include an appendix including reference material.

We have already suggested an audit of design and technology and the construction of an action plan. In Figure 7.1 you can find a format for an action plan.

The first steps in policy writing

You need to find out what the present picture is with regard to the teaching of and achievement in design and technology. You need to know what resources are used by teachers. You also need to know in some detail how design and technology will fit into the school development plan. Does design and technology feature in the plan yet? If so, does it include the right priorities? If not you need to review and plan it carefully with the head and senior management team. These first steps are crucially important, a thorough audit or review will assist as will dialogue with the head or a designated member of the senior management team.

It will also be useful at this time to find as much background information to the subject as possible through books (see the bibliography and list of useful publications), schemes, resources, publications, local courses, professional associations, local support centres, the internet and universities.

A major objective is to begin work with your colleagues, in most cases this will involve a staff meeting or more likely, a series of staff meetings. These might occur in a series of three or four meetings during a half term or, alternatively, you might plan one or two meetings in a term to be followed by others in six or twelve months.

You should be ready to present colleagues with the major issues and listen to their views. You might be better to go for general awareness raising before presenting elements of a draft policy. For more advice about running staff meetings see Cross and Cross (1994), Eason (1985) or Leyland (1988).

On p. 107 you will find an exemplar policy statement for design and technology. This is provided as an example, but there is no doubt that you will have to change it quite significantly to reflect the views of your colleagues and the particular emphases of your school. Do not be surprised if there are suggestions in Figure 8.1 which appear to be impossible in your school at present. It may be that some sections are not appropriate to your school or that this is a measure of the development required. Some items may need to go into the action plan now, prior to inclusion in the policy. It is also likely that you will change the order of headings so as to better reflect your priorities. Equally, you may see a need for sections which do not appear here, the more you can make your policy your own the better.

An opening policy statement

A clear, agreed statement of what you as a staff mean by design and technology education will assist readers and yourselves when you come to make policy decisions later on. It will assist you as coordinator if you can be assured that your work is in line with this statement.

As you see it is impossible to use the text directly, some items may require staff training prior to their inclusion.

This opening statement should not duplicate the detail of what is to follow, rather it sets out the most important issues. The above statement is a fictitious example like the material below.

The policy document

The main policy document will follow an opening statement like the one above and will give, section by section, the advice that a new teacher needs to implement design and technology in the classroom in your school. You should date the document so that its history is clear. The presentation should be as good as you can reasonably make it — word processed and well printed. Keep it as short as possible and keep the current version in hardcopy and in a computer word processor format.

IG 8.1

A statement of policy for design
and technology

> ## Policy Statement for Design and Technology
>
> Design and technology is an important part of the education at .... school.
> All children in the school study design and technology through practical, challenging
> and yet safe activities based initially on their immediate personal experiences and
> later on a broader range of contexts and materials and developing more sophisticated
> techniques and skills.
>
> Design and technology involves children examining the needs of people in a situation
> like building a house, this is an example of a meaningful context. The context of
> the work is most important in design and technology. Design and technology asks
> them to design and plan ways of solving particular problems which they have
> identified i.e. designing a garden with young children in mind; making the product
> (which might be a model garden) and finally evaluating their work. Teachers'
> choice of context will be guided by the scheme of work and will be sensitive to the
> range of children's backgrounds, both economic and cultural.
>
> We believe that all children benefit from design and technology in terms of its
> contribution to their overall capability and from the way that design and technology
> links with other areas of the curriculum like science, English, mathematics, art and
> history.
>
> Our scheme of work ensures that the children cover all of the requirements of the
> National Curriculum. There is a particular emphasis on designing and making which
> goes on within these aspects of design and technology:
> - construction materials;
> - textiles;
> - food.
>
> Teachers are given advice about the different types of tasks children must
> experience: these include focused practical tasks; activities where children
> investigate, disassemble and evaluate simple products and design and make
> assignments.
>
> We consider that attitude to work is very important and so place considerable
> emphasis on the quality of the products and of the process of work. We know
> that children produce their best work when they are interested, therefore, we go to
> considerable effort to make the design and technology work as realistic as possible,
> i.e. we ensure that the children are clear about and have a say in the challenge
> they set themselves. Where possible children make usable products.
>
> Children's achievement in design and technology is constantly reviewed by individual
> teachers and the children. Annual reviews are conducted by the subject's
> coordinator and the whole staff.
>
> date ....

Contents

You should include a list of contents of this policy with reference to the major topics and relevant page numbers.

A brief statement about the status of this document

Very briefly what is the recent history of this document.

 The history of this policy

This policy document for design and technology was written in .... it was reviewed in .... when there was clarification on assessment, recording and reporting and amendments to the topics covered.

Names and roles of those involved in the management of the subject

This is necessary and will assist you in that your role and the contribution of others will be spelt out, thus the limits of your role will be clear.

 Responsibility for the subject

The design and technology teacher coordinator is .... Support is provided by .... who was the previous design and technology teacher coordinator and who provides specific advice and support on Key Stage 2.

Outline of experience you intend that children should have

This is not the scheme of work. Rather, you are making clear the nature of the design and technology. Emphasise practical work where the children take an increasing amount of control of the task.

 Children's experience in design and technology should include a high proportion of practical work. Children are engaged by stimulating contexts, challenges and materials. Children are encouraged to see that design and technology is a part of the life of all cultures and peoples both now and in the past, that we can all participate in design and technology. They should find design and technology enjoyable, meaningful and challenging. They should be given increasing opportunity to control their work.

Planning

Here you need to show that design and technology is part of the whole-school whole-curriculum planning. Time allocation is a whole-school issue that involves you as design and technology coordinator. Reference to your scheme of work is most likely to need to differ from the example that follows. The biggest variable is the extent of freedom to determine tasks which you give to teachers. This will be a reflection of the whole-school approach to this freedom, but does sometimes vary a little in design and technology. Do your colleagues want broad guidance with a little direction or do they want to be told which activity to do, what to say and how to do it?

Planning

Teachers plan design and technology for three half terms in the school year, as per the scheme of work. Plans include a series of learning objectives drawn from the relevant pro-gramme of study. Teachers plan to include focused practical tasks, investigation tasks and at least one design and make task for example in year 3, term 2 .... . Plans should include introductory stimulus, skills and knowledge teaching, a clear role for the teacher, opportunity for teacher assessment, self-assessment by the children and safety.

Time allocation

At Key Stage 1 the time spent on design and technology in one year will be 36 hours and at Key Stage 2 45 hours. At Key Stage 1 this time will often be used in a series of afternoon sessions of 1hr 30mins. At Key Stage 2 there will be a balance of sessions of around 40mins and half days devoted to design and technology. The teacher will ensure that these hours are covered over the year and will report when this has not been possible.

Scheme of Work

A scheme of work for design and technology builds from the whole-school curriculum plan and can be found in the appendix. . . . It gives directions about the nature of the activ-ities which are required and the topics which will form a con-text for the activity. There is reference to the sections of the Programme of Study, vocabulary and basic skills which are required.

Progression

Progression in design and technology has in the past proved somewhat elusive to some teachers. It may therefore be worth specific mention in your policy and explicit inclusion in the scheme of work.

> *Progression*
>
> *We expect all children to progress in design and technology in a number of areas. These will include progressively:*
>
> - *less familiar contexts;*
> - *longer tasks;*
> - *more complex tasks;*
> - *more techniques;*
> - *new techniques;*
> - *techniques being used in combinations;*
> - *working as part of a team;*
> - *identifying criteria for evaluation;*
> - *more accuracy;*
> - *making more informed choices about tools, techniques and materials.*
>
> *The scheme of work is designed so that in each key stage children have the opportunity to return to materials and skills spirally. The scheme of work refers to designing skills, making skills, vocabulary, IT, which ensures that children do return to aspects of the subject within the meaningful contexts offered by the topics.*

Teacher assessment

In order that the teaching of design and technology and its reporting to others including parents is well informed, teachers must include assessment as part of the teaching process. It is this teacher assessment which will lead to informed decisions about differentiation.

> *Assessment*
>
> *Assessment in design and technology proceeds on the basis of teacher assessment and children's self assessment. As in the school's assessment policy the day to day assessment proceeds, based on sound planning where specific learning objectives and related outcomes and criteria for assessment are identified. Teachers share the objectives and the criteria with the children and ask the children to make self-assessments in accordance*

with the child's age and development (a number of relevant proforma are provided for different age ranges, see the appendix). These children's self assessments are added to and validated by the teachers' regular assessment.

❡ *Moderation*

In line with the school's policy for assessment there will be a biannual internal moderation exercise where the design and technology coordinator (in collaboration with the school's AR&R coordinator) collects samples of work from colleagues. Teachers are asked to give judgments as to which level is represented by this work. Consideration of this material will be made during a specified staff meeting where teachers have the chance to discuss such judgments. This will, where possible, be in advance of annual report writing.

Differentiation

Sometimes overlooked in design and technology, differentiation is as important as in any other subject (see Chapter 5), however, teachers must not differentiate for the sake of it. It is recognised that there are times when undifferentiated class lessons are acceptable, for example at the beginning of a topic, and that within a lesson there may be an undifferentiated start, followed by an activity which contains differentiation by outcome or task. Teachers should be encouraged to make good use of differentiation by outcome and to realise that with differentiation by outcome it is **their reaction** to the outcome by the child which is the most important thing! That is, how does their understanding of the child's response affect subsequent teaching and tasks?

❡ *Differentiation*

In our teaching of design and technology we will use differentiation by outcome and differentiation by task in roughly equal proportions as advised by the school's teaching and learning policy. It is suggested that we consider differentiation by outcome in the early activities (focused practical and investigation tasks), followed by task differentiation (focused practical, and investigation tasks) and conclude with an open ended task which differentiates by outcome. Teachers are encouraged to adapt this plan but to ensure the inclusion of its constituents. Differentiation in design and technology can also be planned for in:

- *the time teachers give to individuals and groups;*
- *instructions adults give;*
- *the support adults give;*
- *the expectations teachers have of the children;*
- *the time allowed for the activity;*
- *the material and tools provided;*
- *the range of choice available.*

Teachers should make a professional decision about which handful, or one, of these they might employ in a lesson.

Special needs

Emphasis here is on the fact that design and technology is for all children, including those who have specific learning or behavioural difficulties and others who achieve very well. Much will depend on the school's definition of special needs. These children are the ones who fall out of the expected norms. That is, the differentiation that you might expect to provide cannot provide fully for them.

Special needs

Design and technology can offer all children an exciting and challenging way to learn. Some children might find access to the subject a challenge because of specific sensory impairment, motor control, cognitive limits, behavioural difficulties or a combination of these. Teachers may refer to the school's special needs policy and SENCO. These children may need more than the regular range of differentiation in the class.

Bilingual children

Bilingualism and multilingualism is a special talent and should be celebrated as such. These children however, may experience difficulties with subjects like design and technology particularly if English is not their first language. Design and technology may be viewed by these children with some relish as they may be able to work freely without the constraints of an unfamiliar language.

Bilingualism or multilingualism

Bilingualism or multilingualism is valued as an achievement. As primary teachers of design and technology we should ensure that such children are not impeded by their lack of familiarity with vocabulary. Teachers must ensure that their expectations are not affected by the child's use of language. Teachers might provide differentiated support.

Resources

This section should refer to the teachers' books and materials which you may have to support teaching.

Resources

A teacher's resource is provided in room .... The school has purchased elements of the .... scheme and the .... set of books sufficient to support the topics chosen. These should be available in your classroom or from the design and technology coordinator.

A section has been established in the children's library on design and technology. All of these books should be available in the longer school holidays, please see .... about availability.

Teachers should consider how they can use Information Technology to help them teach design and technology either in terms of planning, presentation or recording. The school's IT coordinator or design and technology coordinator can assist here.

Teaching approaches

The approach to teaching design and technology should be in line with the school teaching policy.

Teaching Approaches

In line with the school's teaching and learning policy there will be a mix of class teaching and group work. Generally teachers should consider class teaching on occasions when it is the most effective way to put ideas over. Group work will be used when there is need for concentrated teacher adult input or on occasions where resources (including space) dictate group work (in these cases the coordinator should be informed as we hope to provide sufficient resources for all teaching styles).

Where teachers have classroom assistance which is directed at design and technology the teacher remains in overall charge and must therefore give clear instructions to the assistant about learning objectives, expectations, outcomes and teaching style.

The class teacher must monitor the quality of the assistant's contribution and give appropriate feedback and advice.

Teaching will feature: clear explanations, summaries, demonstrations, illustrations, examples, challenges etc.

Cross-curricular links

The context of the design and technology is very important and must be stressed. Here you might include one or two examples from the scheme of work or refer the reader to the scheme of work.

❝ *Cross-curricular links*
As we are concerned that children see design and technology as part of their world we are keen to use positive cross-curricular links. By this we mean that the link furthers the objectives of either design and technology or the subject it is linked with or both. You will find an example on page. . . .

Spiritual, moral, social and cultural development

Design and technology can make a particular contribution to spiritual, moral, social and cultural development. It allows children to look at the made objects around them, including ones which they have made, and examine them critically. In this context the children might consider wastage of materials, pollution, cost, availability and even questions about ownership and sharing. Human ingenuity and creative capacity might for example be contrasted with the capacity to destroy.

❝ *Spiritual, moral, social and cultural development*
We consider design and technology to be a useful vehicle for children to consider serious questions about human activity e.g. . . . Achievement in design and technology can positively affect children's self-steem and offer opportunities for socialisation as children work together. Design and technology draws on contributions from all human cultures where children consider people in their work, at home and at play, solving problems with design and technology.

Safety

It is most important to give teachers specific advice here. It is likely that you will need to provide more information in an appendix or subject file. There is specific advice which you would want to give regarding construction materials and tools, textile's tools and food technology. You might include the ASE booklet 'Be Safe' or the NAAIDT booklet 'Make it Safe' as an appendix for each teacher.

 Safety

We consider safety to be an integral part of all our teaching including design and technology. With younger or less mature children there will be a need for the teacher to take responsibility for all safety issues. As children mature it will be possible to talk to them more about safety and to ask them to conduct a safety review of an activity. Children should progressively be expected to take responsibility for safety, but always within their capability and after careful instruction about the use of, for example, tools and materials. Specific advice about the use of tools and materials and food technology is given in ....

Supervision is important in some aspects of design and technology, this should be varied according to the activity. If in doubt please see the design and technology coordinator.

Risk assessment should be carried out for all design and technology activities for this please use the checklist or proforma on page .... .

Equal opportunities

Design and technology is a subject for all human kind, independent of gender, race, culture, religion, ability, disability or economic position. Your policy must be unequivocal about this.

Design and technology is taught in line with the school's equal opportunity policy. We believe that design and technology is an important aspect of everyone's life now and in the future. Design and technology education should account for children's abilities, gender, culture, religion so that it celebrates similarity and difference, ensures access and presents positive images.

Multicultural issues

Tensions within a multicultural society reflect the range of values in that society including prejudice. Design and technology is about the made world and thus is a powerful vehicle for the promulgation of values. You might want your policy to clearly state that as a school you intend to use opportunities from different cultures in the present day and in the past to emphasise similarity and richness in the human community.

> *Multicultural opportunity in design and technology*
> *The school recognises that children receive strong messages about different cultures through technology, i.e. messages about western culture and the value placed on certain products and other cultures which appear to value other things. Western value and dependence on the car may appear to be valued more highly than another culture which uses animals for transport. In design and technology we can look at the similarity of human need and the similarity and difference of the solutions with some evaluation of the solution depending on criteria — the car does well when judged on a criteria of speed (assuming the road is clear!), the car does less well judged against a criteria to do with a sustainable technology.*

Monitoring and evaluation

This is dealt with in some detail in Chapter 11. The place of monitoring and evaluating should be clearly stated here as the assessment of the children's achievement is an important part of the process of monitoring and evaluation.

> *Monitoring and evaluation*
> *Monitoring and evaluation in design and technology is based on the school's approach to monitoring and evaluation of the non-core areas of the National Curriculum. Class teachers monitor the achievement of the children through teacher assessment and their own teaching through regular self-review. Class teachers review their teaching of design and technology each half-term and report to the design and technology coordinator or a member of the schools's senior management. This feedback is combined with evidence which the design and technology coordinator gains from visits to classrooms and sampling of children's work as well as informal observation and discussions with teachers. Teacher assessment of children's work is seen as a major vehicle for determining the effectiveness of the school's design and technology programme. An annual review*

is held by the coordinator and at least one member of the senior management team, with opportunities for colleagues to participate. The general results of this monitoring and evaluation is then reported to the staff so that discussion and action can follow to further improve the children's achievement.

Recording

 Recording

As the children are encouraged to self-assess, this forms the basis of the recording of children's experience and achievement. A range of proforma are provided in the appendix for different age ranges. Children build up over the course of a year a portfolio of work. At the end of the year they are expected to select a representative sample of their recent work and records to show to the next teacher. The teacher will keep records in terms of plans which confirm that the expected curricular coverage has occurred or not. Specific records must be kept of children who fall out of the 'expected' range of achievement (above or below) or who through absence perhaps have missed significant elements of design and technology. These children are, or might at some point be, considered as having some form of special need in design and technology. In line with school policy these records will be passed on to the next teacher in July at a 'pass the class conference' where the teachers will be given an hour to discuss the needs and achievement of the class.

Reporting

 Reporting

Parents receive reports three times a year, twice at parents' meetings (October and June) and once in a written report. On these occasions we encourage parents to look at their children's work and to look at the child's profile which should show progression.

Resources

Here you should refer to a list of resources so that teachers can find the right resources in the right quantity at the right time (there is detail on resourcing in Part 5).

❝ *We are committed to build up the school's resources for design and technology. (See school development plan.) These are available in two central stores. The first is situated ..... and contains the .... and the .... resources. The second houses the .... trolley and contains the ...... resources (see list in appendix ...). In addition, each class contains a set of resources listed in appendix .... The care of this set is the responsibility of the class teacher who will be assisted when the sets are collected, checked and if possible replenished three times a year.*

The whole-school curriculum plan includes design and technology in a pattern which should mean that tools are sufficient for the needs of classes. There is also guidance in the scheme about which tools each class should be using.

The school is presently building up its stock of .... resources for design and technology. Teachers are encouraged to make suggestions which can be considered for the annual bid for design and technology resources. Spending has been confirmed for design and technology for the years ....

There is specific reference to design and technology in the school's IT policy. Core IT applications for design and technology are included in the scheme of work for design and technology.

Staff development

This is likely to be a most important area for design and technology.

❝ *Staff development*

The development of staff is an important part of the school's approach to improve standards of achievement and teaching in design and technology. Annual and other reviews which take place will include teachers' training needs. Particular emphasis will be given to those needs which relate to aspects to be taught by a particular teacher. A programme of training in .... is to be implemented in .... Teachers' materials and information about support and courses are available from the design and technology coordinator .... and the school coordinator of Continuing Professional Development.

Review of the policy

 Policy review

This will occur on a biannual basis following two cycles of annual monitoring and evaluation of the design and technology in the school. All teachers will be consulted about this and there will be a short report to staff on the results. This may lead to discussion, awareness raising, training and ultimately amendments to practice and policy. All members of staff are encouraged to see the design and technology coordinator at any point where they recognise an issue about the achievement of children or the teaching of the subject.

Who is the policy for?

It is important to keep the purpose of the policy and its audience in mind. Directly, the policy is to be used by the teaching staff, or that the practice it describes is to be used by the teachers. The policy is for the governors as they must be assured that the school is fulfilling its legal obligations. The policy is for visiting inspectors, who will need to find evidence that you are engaging the complex task of teaching high quality design and technology. Importantly, the policy is for parents — can you make the policy available to parents? Are policies posted on a noticeboard? Can you refer to policy in communications with parents? Remember that if you are going to make documentation available to parents you ought to avoid jargon. The policy is also for you as design and technology coordinator, if it does represent what is going on in the school it should be a tangible product of your work. It will be a constant contribution to your legitimate expectation that design and technology achievement by the children and teaching by colleagues be taken seriously.

Reviewing the policy

As was said at the start, you might take a design and technology approach to the development of the teaching of design and technology, thus you need to be able to evaluate your progress. It is not the policy document that is under review, it is the policies you are using in the school as represented by the document. This is a strategic review, is your policy having the effects that you want it to? How will you ensure further improvement in children's progressive achievement?

To determine an answer to this question you must conduct regular, periodic evaluation, based on information from monitoring. These ought to be annual or biannual and should be thorough, asking searching, evaluative questions and gathering useful information.

Possible questions would ask to what extent:
- are all children achieving?
- are there any patterns of under-achievement, high achievement?
- how does achievement relate to previous years and other children in the age range?
- are the aims for design and technology sufficient?
- is the planning (long, medium, short term) achieving those aims?
- does teacher expertise promote high achievement and progression?
- does design and technology reflect overall school policies?
- does design and technology link with curricular and other aspects of the school?
- do teachers feel enabled by the support and resources available?

Part of the review should include a review of your own role. You might invite colleagues to give their view or there may be a system for the review of subject coordination in the school. You certainly ought to carry out some self-review, in which case you might consider the headings in Part 2 of this book which relate to what you need to know and what you need to be able to do. Remember that as in any evaluation you are looking for positive aspects as well as negative ones and that the picture is rarely wholly positive or wholly negative but somewhere in between. What you must do is discuss your review with someone who understands the role but who shares your desire to see you develop and is ideally in a position to assist you with identified needs.

Chapter 9

Developing and maintaining a scheme of work for design and technology

Introduction

For classteachers the scheme of work will be the most regularly used piece of documentation for the subject of design and technology. It is here that classteachers will come for the guidance about long and medium term objectives. It is therefore essential that you as design and technology coordinator ensure that the scheme of work furthers all the objectives of design and technology. You should see the scheme as a very powerful tool with which you can promote the subject and children's high achievement in it.

Long term plans

These will include the National Curriculum programme of study plus anything else that you want to include. Extras you might include would reflect your school's interest and might include Information Technology opportunities, attitudes, links with other subjects and cross-curricular dimensions like environmental education. They will aim to ensure coverage of the requirements and balance and breadth within the subject.

Medium term plans

These will break down the long term plans into units which can fit into the school curricular plan. These plans often base themselves around the six half terms of the school year. Many schools employ shorter blocks of time: three weeks for shorter units of teaching and in some cases longer blocks where they run a topic or topics together over a period of a whole term. Primary schools remain wholly or partly wedded to the idea of themes or topics. Where these are well planned they provide an excellent vehicle for promoting achievement in a meaningful context where linked aspects of subjects complement and enrich one-another.

In Figure 9.1 we can see a whole-school plan from Clarendon Road Primary School, Salford which was based on the Guidance and Scheme of Work for Design and Technology produced by Wirral LEA. The school is part-way along the road to a plan which will include all materials in design and technology as they have yet to include food technology in this plan. Food technology occurs in the school and will soon be incorporated into a similar plan. The school has, with this plan, identified a number of design and technology themes or units which mean that there is a guarantee that specific elements of design and technology will be covered. The boxes identify the topic title, suggest an activity or activities, state the kind of activity which will be included, the materials and the aspects of knowledge and understanding from the programme of study.

This is only part of the school's scheme of work, what other information might be included in such a scheme? More detail about themes/topics? Suggested or stipulated activities? A number of schools have then chosen to map out their yearly plan as in the proforma in Figure 9.2.

The long and medium term plans are the main systems which will ensure:
- continuity;
- progression;
- coverage;
- breadth;
- depth;
- that children return to concepts and skills in a spiral manner.

Once again the tasks are given or suggested, the skills to be taught are specified, as is the knowledge and understanding.

FIG 9.1
Design and technology
school overview —
Clarendon Primary
School, Salford (based on
Design and technology:
National Curriculum
Guidance and Scheme of
Work — Wirral LEA)

TECHNOLOGY: Whole school overview — Clarendon Road Primary School

These activities form the bulk of the scheme but there will be other technology activities going on in addition.

PRE KS1			
	RANGE OF ACTIVITIES		
YEAR ONE	**WHEELS AND AXLES** P FT DMA M H Make a moving vehicle. Construct the chassis from a box and attach wheels to dowel axles. c r	**LEVERS AND HINGES** P FT DMA FT M Make a face with a moving part — introduce levers. Introduce hinges. fs ss r	**TEXTILES** FT P DMA Q To make a collage using a variety of fabrics and materials — use of fabric crayons. t
YEAR TWO	**TEXTILES** P FT FT DMA S Make a bag for a purpose. t	**MOVING TOYS ①** P FT DMA P FT M Use construction kits to investigate simple movement. c ss	**MOVING TOYS ②** FT DMA P M S Construct a moving toy related to the FAIRGROUND. H c fr r fs
YEAR THREE	**MOVING VEHICLE** P FT DMA S Make a moving vehicle from framework material. H em fr ss c	**LINKAGES** P FT FT DMA FT M Introduce a range of simple linkages. fs ss c	**INSTRUMENT FOR MEASURING WEATHER** DMA FT P M Design and make an S anemometer. C fr r fs
YEAR FOUR	**PULLEYS** P FT DMA M Make a pulley device. H c fr ss em r	**3D CUBE** P FT DMA S Make a 3D cube. Introduce corner joints. Use appropriate materials to make a house. fr rs	**SCREEN PRINTING** DMA FT P Q Design a stencil. Use screen and ink to print onto cotton. t
YEAR FIVE	**FASTENINGS** P FT DMA Examine a collection of safety clothes. Investigate fastenings. t	**HYDRAULICS** FT FT DMA M Introduce pneumatics and H hydraulics using syringes to push/pull, lift/lower, open/ close. em ss	**MASKS** P FT DMA Make a mask using a variety of textile techniques. t mo
YEAR SIX	**GEARS AND CAMS** P FT FT DMA M Investigate gears. Make a turning toy. Introduce cams. fr c ss em	**MOTORISED VEHICLE** P FT FT DMA S Use a 2D frame to M construct a motorised vehicle. c fr ss em	**BRIDGES** P FT DMA S Investigate structures M Make a bridge with a moving C part H em fr ss c

ACTIVITIES	DMA Design and Make Assignment		FT Focused Task	P Products and Applications	
MATERIALS	c construction kits	fr framework	ss stiff sheet	t textiles	r reclaimed
	fs flexible sheet	f food	em electrical/mechanical		mo mouldable
KNOWLEDGE AND UNDERSTANDING	M mechanisms	S structures	C control	Q quality	H health and safety

* The three activities for each year group may be completed in any order.

* Food activities are to take place at least once each school year.

Design and Technology
time allocation for the year .... hrs

Year ....

topic	term	topic	term	topic	term
....	....	....	....	....	....
tasks		tasks		tasks	
materials		materials		materials	

skills	tools	skills	tools	skills	tools

vocabulary		vocabulary		vocabulary	

knowledge & understanding		knowledge & understanding		knowledge & understanding	
IT		IT		IT	

FIG 9.2
Proforma for the medium term plans of design and technology

By specifically stating which tools will be used and introduced there is an explicit statement of progression. In implementing anything like this a number of issues have to be resolved with colleagues:

- how much of this guidance is advisory and how much compulsory?
- how will the nursery and reception class fit in?
- does all design and technology have to fit in with the topic?
- do the three (or whatever number) activities have to be done in an order?
- do colleagues understand the associated terminology?
- do colleagues have sufficient background knowledge?
- what support will be available?
- will you be able to avoid duplication of resources?
- returning to areas in a spiral approach may be possible at Key Stage 2 (4 years), is it possible in Key Stage 1?
- when will it be reviewed?

Short term planning

Here the teacher will take the medium term objectives and turn them into concrete plans for the classroom. In some cases schools have worked together to write these and have for design and technology used similar plans in subsequent years. This is possible for generic activities, but there does need to be some flexibility for the different children that we might come across.

The proforma in Figure 9.3 will become a record of work completed by the class and of achievement for a proportion of the children. Such a proforma might be given to the next classteacher to provide extra information. The section on outcomes could give an essential summary of the response of the children.

Activity Plans for Design and Technology		Class .... Term .... Year				
activity number	activity (IDE, FPT or DMT?)	objectives	differentiation	assessment opportunity/criteria	safety	resources/ materials

outcomes

© Falmer Press Ltd.

FIG 9.3
Proforma for short term activity plans in design and technology

Chapter 10

More than maintaining

Introduction

Maintaining an area of the curriculum can only mean moving forward. It has been said by more than one person that if a primary school is not moving forward it can only move backward, there is no state of equilibrium. This is futher emphasised when you note that all around a school and a subject there is movement. The curriculum changes as do ideas about teaching and, of course, the children. In order to keep pace with change we must be constantly developing our school and our subject.

A continuous staff conference

Design and technology is an area where staff are often willing to admit that they don't know much and are willing to learn, therefore, they are ready to listen and take ideas on. Thus it is an area for teamship.

Running events for the teachers

As design and technology coordinator you will have to organise meetings, workshops etc. for the staff. You need to think about your experience in doing these things and about your confidence:

- Are there colleagues in school who do this sort of thing?
- How do they go about it?
- Would they give you some advice?

You must consider the extent to which you feel happy running different sessions:

- What about preparing an agenda and running a meeting?
- How can you stimulate discussion?
- What should you prepare?
- How much discussion will you need?

Relationships

Relationships with colleagues are an important part of the development of the subject. As a younger member of staff you may find yourself advising colleagues with more experience, so you need to be sensitive to tensions that may arise. You will need to show that while you have not got the experience of, for example, teaching that particular age range, you are willing to assist as far as you can and to learn. Communication, being a two-way process, will be your greatest ally. Make sure you establish communication at a number of levels — about different aspects of school life, including design and technology and life outside school. You will be constantly assessing the needs of your colleagues and the evidence you gather will include observations of their classroom and children's work, but simply listening to the teachers will tell you much of what you need to know. Listening to others is an important skill to develop.

School liaison

Liaison with other schools is rarely top of the priority list for primary schools. Perhaps some see it as the prerogative of the receiving school. Recent changes like local management do not appear to encourage schools to collaborate, senior management have got to see the advantages for the children. Where a primary school feeds to more than two or three high schools there will be a limit to the time you can devote to liaison with each school yet pupils can gain considerably from liaison between the teachers of their primary and high school. It might help to think in terms of the following levels and to note that any contact is far better than none at all.

Everyone needs to be clear from the start that it is a two-way process, there are professional skills in both schools and colleagues from each phase of education, who stand to gain from contact with pupils and colleagues in the other phase.

As design and technology coordinator you ought at some point to introduce yourself to the head of department for design and technology at the high school. If you are coordinating in a junior or infant school you will have to promote liaison with colleagues in the primary phase. You need to seek opportunities to get to know the staff and vice versa.

Levels of liaison	Possible design and technology examples
meeting together simple contact, getting to know each other	– teachers visit schools in or out of hours – teachers attend open events – teachers receive school brochures – equipment is loaned – attend open events in the other school
talking together recognition that we will start to work together	– teachers attend and may get involved in lessons – meetings attended by staff from both schools – primary pupils visit high school for lesson/s – primary records are taken seriously
collaboratively working together teachers start to work together	– joint events i.e. training, exhibitions, competitions – systematic visits in both directions – sharing of equipment – bridging topic (starts in year 6 and is completed in year 7)

If you recognise any things above that you do already or can identify others then you have made a start. Liaison is rarely self-maintaining, it requires commitment from senior management and teachers to a two-way transfer of ideas and information which should assist the children.

In your monitoring of the subject and your role, do look at liaison; how much time is devoted to it? What return are you seeing for this effort? Are there tangible benefits? Could your senior management assist you? It is important that there are positive outcomes.

The last form of liaison occurs between primary schools in an area or an LEA. Is there opportunity for design and technology coordinators to meet? Is the LEA interested in assisting? Can you use the internal LEA mail to advertise your interest?

Action research and teachers

Action research which is often part of degree and higher degree courses for teachers is not only to be used by academics. Teachers can pose questions about their practice and their children's learning and attainment. They can plan a simple enquiry which will provide them with more information and lead them towards analysis of what they observe. Such activity can often lead you to discover dimensions in a classroom about which you were unaware that might include behaviours, levels of achievement, interactions. All of these things influence achievement in subjects like design and technology. Primary design and technology needs a foundation of teacher research. For more information on this type of simple enquiry read Judith Bell's book *Doing Your Research Project* (1987).

Resource development

Design and technology is affected by resource provision. It cannot rely wholly on reclaimed materials. Primary schools need to provide resources for design and technology. Ofsted inspectors stated in 1995 that in the previous year the average spent per child on design and technology was £2.50, though this varied in some schools from 20 pence per child to over £10 per child in others. Senior managers should be made aware of the importance of resources to design and technology. If the school does not provide a range of materials in contsruction and textiles there will be a detrimental effect on the children's achievement.

As well as being concerned about the amount of money being spent, you should be looking at areas of design and technology which you do not yet cover or aspects which might benefit from

Parental involvement

As the subject develops you might find growing interest from parents. Where this is not the case you may want to ensure that parents become aware of the subject. For many different reasons you might decide to organise a parents' workshop, display or open event of some kind. There may be a precedent in the school of similar events so talk to other coordinators. Decide on the time and date of such an event:

- what will be the objective?
- decide whether you want children to be present
- will someone give a short explanatory talk?
- what sort of activities will be going on?
- if children are present what will be their role?

a new resource. You will need to keep aware of developments in equipment and materials so that you are in a position to put a bid together quickly.

Parental involvement

You might want to run training sessions for parents, either as general awareness raising sessions, confidence building sessions, sessions showing how they can help in the classroom or how they can help their own child at home. Outside consultants will often give advice or help with the organisation of this type of event.

Some parents will not be able to join you at school and you may need to consider other ways to communicate with them. Some kind of newsletter might assist. Some schools have a half termly note for parents from each class about topics to be covered and activities parents and children might do at home. A design and technology competition would communicate certain messages about the subject.

Part four Monitoring for Quality

Chapter 11

A holistic view of monitoring and evaluating

Introduction

Monitoring and evaluation of design and technology needs to be approached in a positive manner. It is about establishing the effectiveness of the school by forming judgments about the extent to which children are achieving or not! Your monitoring and evaluation should include sufficient detail for you to identify the stronger points of design and technology in the school as well as the weaker points. Primary teachers may find it quite a challenging subject, therefore it will be important to know that our hard work is well targeted.

The role of subject coordinator is a challenging one, monitoring and evaluation represents perhaps the most challenging aspect of that role. It will require you to view the whole school, to observe, to be professional and objective. Monitoring and evaluation should put you in the position of knowing much about what is going on in design and technology and most importantly what the results of the school's efforts really are.

Subject coordinators with limited experience, for example those who have never taught junior aged children, often feel nervous about making judgments about the teaching and learning in that age range. Young coordinators may feel apprehensive about judging any aspect of the work of more senior or long serving colleagues. These feelings are quite understandable and require sensitivity on everyone's part. This does not, however, take away from the fact that someone has got to gain a view of design and technology in the whole school. Prior to your doing this, no-one will have had such a detailed view. The process should empower everyone.

The two words **monitoring** and **evaluating** are used freely in education and lose their meaning on occasions when they merge into one word 'monitoringandevaluation'. The two words have different meanings. **Monitoring** is about determining whether agreed policies are being implemented. **Evaluation** uses evidence from monitoring to determine whether those policies are the right ones to achieve the stated objectives (Russell, 1994). Thus we must have aims for the subject and a policy. The words monitoring and evaluation are particularly pertinent in a subject like design and technology which, as we have seen, includes within the subject the important notion of evaluation, evaluating the products of design and technology.

Monitoring and evaluation in school are whole-school issues and as such are issues for the school's senior management team. Monitoring and evaluation of the curriculum is an essential part of quality control for the school and so there ought to be a whole-school policy on this and as a subject coordinator you will be expected to contribute. A plan for monitoring and evaluating design and technology could relate to a whole-school policy and you need to make it an explicit part of your role. It might, for example, feature in your action plan.

Monitoring can be seen as establishing the extent to which policy and practice match. We have suggested an initial audit of the subject, that would be a start to the monitoring process. We will come to evaluation a little later.

Monitoring design and technology

You need a systematic approach and in order to progress you need to have:

- a clear view of the purpose of design and technology education;
- a clear view of your role in monitoring and evaluating;
- a clear focus on the need to maintain or raise standards;
- delegated responsibility from the headteacher.

and be able to look at:
- the whole-school curriculum plan;
- documentation for design and technology and other subjects and aspects in school;
- resource provision;
- medium and short term plans of teachers;
- teaching;
- children's work;
- children working;
- assessments made by colleagues of children's attainment in design and technology;
- the work of children outside your school.

What am I looking for?

Information gathering is essential to monitoring, first, so that you can form judgments, but second, so that you can give examples from your school of good practice or achievement in the children. Telling a staff that designing needs to be improved will be made more effective through providing one or two examples of good work and helping them to relate this to their own work.

So what am I asking?

You might consider these questions. Is the children's design and technology work:
- within the boundaries of what we might expect from children of this age?
- as such, where does it fall, at the higher end of achievement? at the lower end?
- are there factors affecting the quality of work? adversely? positively?
- are there groups of children achieving in a particular way?
- to what extent, and in what ways, does the planning, organisation and teaching of design and technology affect children's achievement?

As a subject coordinator you are looking for patterns and trends. How are the children performing this year in relation to other years? How are they performing in relation to other children of their age? Is each group (male, female, younger, older, ethnic, cultural, achievement, children at any stage of the special needs process) receiving their entitlement?

Mechanisms for monitoring

The most important step for a school to take is the implementation of a policy for monitoring and evaluating. With such a policy in place you, as design and technology coordinator, will add the design and technology element to the system. Without such a policy you may still have good practice in school which you can follow. You will need to establish which of the things below are available for you to do now, include them in your action plan and begin negotiation for other elements like classroom visits. Be prepared to explain how these will assist your role and try to show afterwards that it leads to positive things.

A whole-school policy

A whole-school policy including a summary such as Figure 11.1, should tell you who does what, when they do it, who is involved, what they look at and to whom they report. The example is from a school which has a whole-school policy and which allocates funding to the process each year. In the case of this school English and mathematics monitoring and evaluation receives more funding than the other subjects. The coordinators of each foundation subject and science can expect to be given release time to see two or three classes per year. This means that they will have observed the whole school every 4–5 years. In choosing which classes to visit the school ensures that each year, each coordinator spreads their attention across the full age range of the school. If you are implementing monitoring and evaluation without a budget for release time you need to look at the items listed here and those in Figure 11.3 which do not require funds. However, you ought to negotiate with the senior management team, perhaps making a special case for design and technology. If no money is available you may have to be satisfied with including it in your long term planning as an objective when funds allow.

who?	what?	how?	when?
all staff	monitor balance, breadth continuity and progression moderation of standards monitor standards of achievement evaluate resource provision evaluate medium term plans	review year planner look at samples of work across Key Stage formal and informal assessments records evaluation sheets	July for the following year 1 staff meeting per half term see AR&R policy at the end of each unit of work (half termly maths and English)
coordinator	monitor subject specific teaching and learning: – policy and practice – standards of achievement – quality of teaching – progression – resource provision	observe teaching and learning review samples of work monitor assessment results evaluation sheets from staff	1 day per term for maths and Eng. 1 day per year for all other subjects see AR&R policy as above
senior management team	policy & schemes reflect current educational developments INSET needs overall responsibility for monitoring and evaluation — long, medium, short term plans for: balance, breadth continuity, progression National Curriculum coverage/ school priorities time allocation standards of achievement quality of teaching & learning	annual audit monitoring short term planning classroom observations evaluate assessment results with coordinators annual audits & target setting with coordinators	spring, prior to School Development Plan & Management Plan weekly once per half term per class see AR&R policy spring/early summer

(1996 SVC)

FIG 11.1
Light Oaks Junior School — monitoring and evaluation systems and procedures

FIG 11.2
Monitoring and evaluating cycle

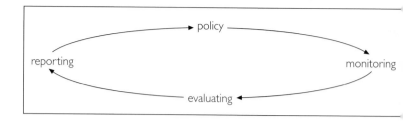

Defining roles

Importantly, the policy states that everyone has a role. In design and technology this starts with the children evaluating their own work and that of others and includes teachers looking at the range and standard of work going on in the classroom. The coordinator is involved, gaining a view about patterns across the whole school. The senior management are involved through looking at patterns across the subject, across other subjects and across aspects of the school. Figure 11.2 shows the cycle of monitoring and evaluating that takes place.

A regular audit

A periodic audit where you go through all your subject paperwork, policy and monitoring activity should assist you in putting together a report. This might occur just prior to a period of monitoring or at the beginning of such a period, but should contribute to a report (see Figure 11.3).

Visiting classrooms

Spending time with teachers and children engaged in design and technology is one of the most valuable actions you can take as design and technology coordinator. It will allow you to gain a detailed picture of what is going on in school. You might think in terms of two to four such sessions in a school year and you should determine the purpose of the visit prior to the visit. It is best to be clear about your desire to assist and, in order to do so, you need to find out what is going on. All of this must be done through the headteacher, and, if it has not occurred before, may take some time to set up. If you are given a choice make your first classroom visit to a teacher who is likely to be positive about the experience.

Audit of design and technology

coordinator ....

date ....

senior manager ....

Relation to the school development plan

	present situation	future action	review date
DOCUMENTATION policy scheme guidelines school development plan			
RESOURCES requirements access storage stock control staff awareness			
MONITORING termly/weekly plans records assessment results classroom visits special needs previous inspection report (& action plan)			
INSET needs courses in school training			
OTHER ISSUES special needs cross-curricular equal opportunities safety			

© Falmer Press Ltd.

FIG 11.3
Audit proforma for design and technology

What is the purpose of classroom visits?

Both you and the classteacher have an agenda, can the visit assist both of you? Negotiate the focus so that you get to see what you want to and the teacher gets the feedback he or she feels that they need. The teacher must know in advance why you are visiting and what you will do. Try to negotiate as much as possible, your purpose is best served by teachers who are as relaxed as possible about this process. Be clear about timing and confidentiality (what will happen to the results).

How will you conduct the observation?

Will you simply sit and watch or will you participate and observe while you work with the children? This may be affected by the focus of your visit, a focus only on teaching may require one particular technique. As you are also interested in the response or achievement of the children you may choose to participate in some way and if you are new to the process you might find it useful to try different approaches or take advice from colleagues. Be honest with colleagues, tell them what you are doing and give the teacher concerned some say in what will go on.

If you are going to participate, consider being involved in something other than design and technology. In a group integration situation you might take a group and so free the teacher for a little more time to spend with the design and technology group. You should be positioned so that you can **see and hear** what is going on. Remember that you are not there to teach, you may need to give your full attention to the observation. Other options are to team teach together or for you to act as teacher's assistant. In both instances you should be in a very good position to observe your colleague and their interactions with the children.

Beware of recording, written notes, tape and video can be used but can make the whole experience much more stressful for your colleague. In the first instance, it may be better to make some agreed notes together at the end of the session.

Try all these options and recognise that they each have advantages and disadvantages. You may be surprised at how soon the children get used to having you there.

Feedback and discussion

Feedback has to be handled carefully. If all is perfect you have an easy job of congratulation. If however, as is more likely, there are points for development you need to approach the teacher in as supportive a way as possible. It would be easy to upset someone who is a little tense about the whole process. As you are acting as a professional friend you need to balance the calm reassuring voice of a friend with a little of the rigour and single mindedness of the professional. All the time you must remind yourself that this teacher has at least ten other subjects to teach and that design and technology is only one of them. If you have concerns, then you will probably need to meet again, so make an arrangement which gives you time to think and pull ideas together. Try to ensure that the teacher gets some kind of positive outcome alongside any areas for consideration.

Alternatives to direct classroom visits

Teacher self-observation

The whole area of teacher research in their own classroom is a very productive one for the direct outcomes and the overall message of reflection and review.

Teacher observation of children

Teacher assessment is a form of systematic observation the intention of which is to determine the extent of children's achievement and progress. Here we suggest that the focus is the teacher's teaching. How are the following used in design and technology?

- teachers' time
- responses
- interventions
- questions
- guiding

Audio tape recording

This is a useful technique in that it allows a great deal of information to be recorded without interfering with the session.

Audio tape recorders are not as intrusive as video recording. Beware — it is easy to record hours of classroom interaction only to find that each hour of tape can take 4–6 hours to analyse. The simplest approach is to play back the tape once or twice for a general impression. A tape recorder with a counter is invaluable as the most interesting interactions can be numbered and easily found at a future date.

Video tape recording

Video tape picks up an audio track as well as the video track and so presents a rich form of evidence. Of course, the camera misses many things. Once again you will find that watching the tape through for overall impressions may be the only practical way of using the recording. Never force video recording on to a teacher. A good way to introduce it is to subject yourself to it first. Another useful option is to guarantee that only the teacher will have access to the video tape.

Looking at assessment results

Results of assessment in design and technology will be a valuable source of information, showing trends and patterns that may exist. Teachers will be looking at children's work and making judgments. The assessment being made by teacher colleagues is a considerable bank of data about what is happening in the school. How many children are being described as above average? How many below? Are children making progress? What proportions of the school population are these? Are there differences between boys and girls? Between children who achieve well in say maths or English? You may want to pose these questions, but no doubt you will soon identify questions of your own.

Eliciting the opinions of colleagues

The opinions of all teachers are not always actively sort. Some teachers give their opinion freely whether asked or not, others may keep their opinion to themselves. They are the most informed group of adults available to you in relation to design and technology in the school. What they tell you about the subject will tell you about how the subject is being taught and pupil achievement. It will also inform you about the teachers' perceptions of the subject and, to some extent, the state of their knowledge of the subject. A short questionnaire has been used in a number of schools to good effect.

Sample questionnaire
1   To what extent have you been able to teach design and technology?
2   How well does design and technology fit into the school's overall plans?
3   How well have the school's design and technology resources met children's needs in lessons?
4   How well does design and technology fit into your classroom?
5   How have the children in your class achieved in design and technology this year?
6   I have had enough time to complete design and technology tasks this year.

You can make the questionnaire easier to fill in by giving teachers a number to circle, e.g.

agree strongly			disagree strongly
1	2	3	4

However short, written answers may give you more information.

Keep the number of questions low. This will mean that you need less time to analyse the data and that teachers will be happy to complete it. They may also be happy next time you offer them a questionnaire! Teachers usually, and understandably, want to know the results of such a survey, you should summarise the results briefly avoiding the temptation to identify individuals.

Don't forget that no matter how good the questionnaire, people will rarely write down all the things they will happily talk about. Some time to simply talk to colleagues about the subject may prove very valuable.

Reviewing teachers' planning

The headteacher and your colleagues may allow you to see teaching forecasts for design and technology. This allows you as coordinator to monitor whether the school's long and medium term plans are being turned into short term plans.

It also allows you to provide specific support and advice in relation to these particular lessons planned by teachers.

Previous inspection reports

If the school has had any kind of inspection, the report should be of interest to you. If it reported on design and technology it may include recommendations and even in cases where the school's design and technology was praised there may be clues in the text to assist you in focusing your attention. If the report did not for some reason mention design and technology you might still be interested in the things that inspectors were looking at; the emphasis on standards, achievement, teaching, parents' attitudes. Where there are explicit references to design and technology, these must be dealt with as anyone following up that report may use previous reports as a starting point.

Keeping your ear to the ground

A less formal approach can give you lots of information about what is actually happening and about teachers' concerns. This means getting out of your room and walking around the school in a relaxed way chatting to colleagues and making general observations, for many coordinators this describes what they do on a weekly basis. For many it will be sufficient to ask:

- how often do I do this?
- do I give myself time to observe?
- do I listen to my colleagues?
- do I visit all parts of school regularly?

This strategy will not be enough on its own, as primary design and technology coordinators, like all full-time primary teachers, are limited in the time that they have to walk around and have no time available when classes are in session.

Examining children's work

This is a most important part of the work of the design and technology coordinator. As you cannot undertake to look at every child's work in design and technology, you must sample. Such a sample should take into account the full age range of the school and the achievement of different children. If you

Ask yourself when examining children's work:
- how does this work relate to the work of other children, is it high, low or average achievement?
- is there a group of children (boys, girls, high ability, a cultural group) whose attainment varies?
- does this work represent progress?

already have arrangements for visiting classes while they are in session you might like to include these classes as part of your sample.

You will need to negotiate access to children's work. Set yourself a minimum number that you hope to see, if you see more that is a bonus. One technique might be to include a sample of six children from across the spread of ability in the class in each of two classes per half term. You might rotate your time around all the classes in the school over a year or two depending on the size of the school. An early focus on the ends of and beginnings of Key Stages will assist your view of the progress children are making. As a year or two go by follow that Year 1 or Year 3 class through, how do they progress? The classteachers will be able to provide additional information. Try to avoid taking more than a few minutes of the teacher's time and work hard at making the teacher see the good things that they and the children are doing.

An important part of this review cycle is that you and the teachers are aware of any elements of design and technology which have either been missed, or to which children responded either very negatively or positively. If this happens mid-year it is the responsibility of the teacher, with your support, to amend future plans to accommodate the children's needs. If this occurs towards the end of the year the information will need to be communicated to the next teacher. You may have a role here.

Visiting other schools

It is essential that you build up a detailed picture of design and technology throughout your school. The value of this information will be limited if you cannot relate it to the wider population of children. It is therefore very worthwhile, when you have built up a reasonable picture of provision, teaching and achievement in your school, to make visits as design and technology coordinator to other primary schools. You may need to explain the purpose of such a visit to the head as well as the potential advantages, as she/he will have to negotiate such visits with other heads. In fact both schools stand to gain. Such visits will allow you to broaden your view of design and technology in the primary years, to compare notes with another design and technology coordinator. Beware of making one visit and jumping to conclusions about your own school, even a group of four or five schools may not be a representative sample of the whole country. However, you will learn interesting things and it will allow you to look afresh at what goes on in your school.

Ground rules for monitoring and evaluation

Agreed whole-school guidelines for this sort of activity are highly desirable. Monitoring and evaluation is the responsibility of the senior management team. They need to establish the framework in which you can operate as a subject manager. If this does not exist, you may be able to go ahead but you need the approval and support of the senior management in order to get release time from your class. You need to agree:

- why this is happening;
- who will be involved and when;
- that information will be dealt with sensitively.

Following any classroom visits you should promptly see the teacher for a short meeting where the two of you agree what happened and where you consider together the aim of the visit. Where you identify a need it is a good idea if you agree a form of words to summarise your conclusion and some action which ideally you can both take. The teacher should realise that you will have to make a summary report to the headteacher. This involvement of the head is essential as it gives the head a clear view of the importance of design and technology and of course it is they who will have to agree to the allocation of resources to assist with any issues. This should all mean that such visits lead to positive outcomes.

If a teacher has allowed you to make observations in their classroom it is important that they get, in their mind, a positive outcome. This could simply be your approval of something they have done well. If you would like to mention something to the head following an observation remember the ethics, ask the teacher's permission. Even positive feedback is feedback and the teacher should agree as to who is going to know what.

Where teachers do not appear to be implementing written policy the written policy should always be questioned. The two must come together, but change may be required at both ends.

Conclusion

This chapter is important as the view held of monitoring and evaluation varies. There is a pervasive culture in some primary schools that since the school is small it is reasonable to say that we all know what is going on. This view is flawed in a number of respects. The most obvious is the focus of each teacher on their own class which mitigates against meaningful time to look at the detail of other groups of children. Another is the social structure of a primary school. The close proximity of colleagues and the intensity of teaching mean that teamship and support are all important. Such needs are not necessarily assisted by the asking of rigorous questions about classroom practice. The approach of the professional friend has much to recommend it.

Chapter 12

Assessment, recording and reporting

Introduction

Assessment is a powerful tool in the armoury of the primary
coordinator of design and technology and, as was seen in
Chapter 5, the contribution of assessment and recording was
emphasised to the school's monitoring and evaluation in
Chapter 11. Assessment, recording and reporting are important
to the design and technology coordinator as assessment will
drive the cycle of teaching and make it responsive to the
needs of the children. It will also, as has been said, provide
an important source of information for both monitoring and
evaluating the design and technology going on in the school.
In order that your advice to colleagues complements other
school policy you should make yourself familiar with the
content of the school Assessment, Recording and Reporting
(AR&R) policy and establish dialogue with the colleague
responsible for this.

Primary teachers are unlikely to have the time to devote to
assessment in design and technology in the way that they do
for numeracy and literacy. For this reason this chapter suggests
an approach to assessment and record keeping that is efficient
and effective. Efficiency, in this context, means avoiding
excessive use of teachers' time, effectively meaning that the efforts
of both teacher and child in the assessment, recording and
reporting of design and technology are focused on ensuring the
child's progressive achievement in the subject. This is important

for you as the coordinator, as you need to offer an approach which is meaningful and attainable by colleagues. It would be easy for you as coordinator to lose credibility and the hearts of teachers if you promote forms of assessment and recording which are time consuming and ineffective!

A distinction is often made between formal and informal assessment. There is no doubt that a great deal of so called 'informal' assessment goes on in primary classrooms. This chapter wishes to value both forms but to rename them informal and systematic. Informal assessment is that which is an outcome of each interaction between the teacher and the child or the child's work. Systematic assessment is not so different as it includes many of the same interactions, but is a form of assessment which is planned for. The teacher may plan so that assessment of design and technology:

- is part of everyday classroom activity in design and technology;
- will provide useful information for future teaching plans;
- has a time allocation;
- is focused on individuals or groups;
- is directed towards particular aspects of design and technology;
- involves the children.

As teachers we need to develop our personal skills for assessment. We need to be able to observe (seeing and hearing), question, summarise, judge, communicate, analyse and use assessment in our planning.

Types of assessment

We have to accept that the history of assessment in primary design and technology is short and that design and technology is likely to make use of all forms of assessment. First, we should remind ourselves of the purpose of assessment and the different types of assessment which have related but different purposes. Teachers need to use **formative assessment** on a day to day basis as children respond to tasks and activities and we as teachers make assessments which will feed back into the plans for subsequent lessons. We need to use **diagnostic assessment** where particular children show problems, i.e. a difficulty with symbols, poor eyesight, poor concentration. Such diagnostic tools might not be associated with design and technology, they are more likely to be amongst the battery of tests and instruments that the school special needs coordinator (SENCO) would have available. It may be that a child's special need might become apparent when asked to conduct a making task. **Summative assessment**, may, on the surface, look no different from teacher assessment, but would be conducted to provide a summary of the child's achievement at the end of a significant stage in education (ages 5, 7 and 11 in primary school). Thus it will allow some judgment about the child's attainment in design and technology and information to the design and technology coordinator about the achievements of the cohort of children. This information can be compared either to other children or the same children's previous achievement.

Such assessment which measures the child against personal previous achievement is known as **ipsative assessment**. This chapter argues that assessment of design and technology should include elements of ipsative assessment. Throughout, the assessment in design and technology by teachers will include **criterion-referenced assessment**. Children will be constantly assessed against criteria — is the child able to develop a design? These criteria will often come from the National Curriculum Programme of Study, either directly or more often derived from the teacher's learning objectives. An element of **norm-referenced** assessment will occur whenever the child is assessed in relation to a wider group of peers. The difficulty here for design and technology is that since the APU research of the 1980's and 90's (Kimbell et al., 1991) there has been no national data against which to reference children's achievement in design and technology.

The assessment to which we refer in this book is often called '**teacher assessment**'. It is so called as it is carried out wholly by teachers in the classroom, largely for the purpose of informing future teaching (formative) but eventually feeding into a summative (end of stage) assessment. In 1992 (SEAC, 1992) several non-compulsory Standard Assessment Tasks were written to be used with 7-year-olds. These remain good examples of teaching and assessment.

FIG 12.1
Steps in teacher assessment

An example of teacher assessment

As assessment is such an important part of the teaching process. We start with the teacher's plans.

teacher action	an example
Teacher identifies element of the National Curriculum Programme of Study to be taught. (Based on the school's long term plans.)	Key Stage 2 Programme of Study children should be taught to: 3c: clarify their ideas, develop criteria for their designs and suggest ways forward. (DfE, 1995)
Formulates these into learning objectives.	1 make their ideas about a maths game clear through a plan 2 write at least one criteria for a good maths game 3 plan the steps of making the maths game
Formulates assessment criteria.	1 describe in a plan or verbally an idea which is clear 2 state or write a criteria which focuses on a characteristic of a good game in the view of the child 3 devise a plan which describes a way forward
Selects a learning activity which will allow the concept to be taught and achievement judged against the criteria.	Design and make a maths game to be used by four and five year olds.
Teacher gathers information during the teaching session.	1 children's written, spoken plans 2 written, spoken criteria
Teacher judges those children who have made expected progress and others.	A group is identified who need significant prompting plus three children whose designing is excellent. The rest achieved in line with expectations.
Teacher considers 'the others' and their achievement.	Perhaps to alter future plans or to cater for some of the class in a differentiated activity.
Teacher uses information formatively in future plans or summatively in a statement of the child's achievement to date.	Information used to plan some differentiation in next task and is fed into the end of year report writing.

A 'child-led' bias

As was said in the introduction to the book, design and technology is about a process which includes designing and making. It requires that children look at existing human made artefacts and evaluate them. It requires that children look at their own designs and products and evaluate them, too. It is suggested here that you build on these reflective strengths of the subject to the point where children are contributing significantly to either self-assessment or keeping their own records, or both.

Children know whether they have used a saw and they know how confident they are in using a saw. Children are, more often than not, over critical of themselves. The few children who are likely to overestimate their capability are usually well known to a primary teacher. This approach has its roots in the record of achievement tradition (SEAC, 1990).

Here we suggest that the teacher utilises strategies to allow children to self-assess their achievement as much as possible with the teacher using informal and systematic teacher assessment to validate (or not) the child's self-assessment.

Strategies

The choice of strategies must be a trade off of advantages and disadvantages. If we had classes of fifteen and were only teaching design and technology we could afford to devote considerable amounts of time to assessment and record keeping in the subject. With nine National Curriculum subjects to assess and record with classes in the mid to high thirties we have to select efficient yet effective strategies. The sub-headings below might be useful as sub-headings in the section of your school policy for design and technology which deals with assessment, recording and reporting.

Sharing the lesson objectives

Being very clear with children about the purpose of a lesson would be considered by many to be normal good practice.

This would assist the children to see where this lesson fits in relation to other lessons and would mean that they might be in a better position at the end of the lesson to make a judgment themselves about their own learning.

The National Curriculum programme of study includes language that even young children can cope with orally, 'make a . . .', 'how will you design a . . .'. By sharing the objectives of the lesson and even your assessment criteria with the children, the children will be able to state whether they feel they have the skill or knowledge. Doing this will take time so should be planned into lessons. It is of course necessary to do this in a positive atmosphere, where admitting that you cannot yet do something is seen as a positive thing.

I can . . . sheets
The proformas in Figure 12.2 are examples of the sort of positive style which you might want to adopt. Here children can make extensive records of their capability, forming perhaps a short term or longer term profile of their achievement.

Design and make proformas

Schools have made extensive use of proformas on which children draw a design and/or plan their action prior to making a product. If children are encouraged to draw freely and to annotate their drawings these activities can reveal much about the children's development.* Teachers who have used them will warn that they provide only part of the picture and cannot be used as the only evidence. Many children do more designing once they have started making, they change a shape, reconsider a material, perhaps learn a new technique for joining. This is much more like the iterative process described by the APU in the introduction to the book (Figure I.3).

Record of achievement

It is most appropriate that over a period of time a portfolio of the child's work is gathered. This might include work selected by the teacher or by the child but should contain work which

* Some schools provide teachers with a bank of similar proformas. These can be Key Stage related thus providing evidence of progression in teaching.

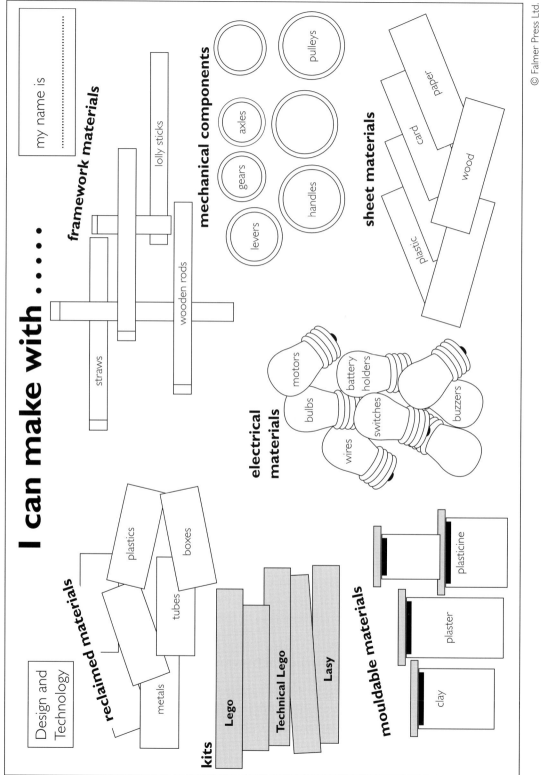

I can make with . . . . .

my name is
....

Design and Technology

framework materials

straws

lolly sticks

wooden rods

mechanical components

levers

gears

axles

handles

pulleys

sheet materials

plastic

card

wood

paper

electrical materials

bulbs

motors

wires

switches

battery holders

buzzers

reclaimed materials

plastics

boxes

tubes

metals

kits

Lego

Technical Lego

Lasy

mouldable materials

clay

plaster

plasticine

(a)

Design and Technology

my name is ....

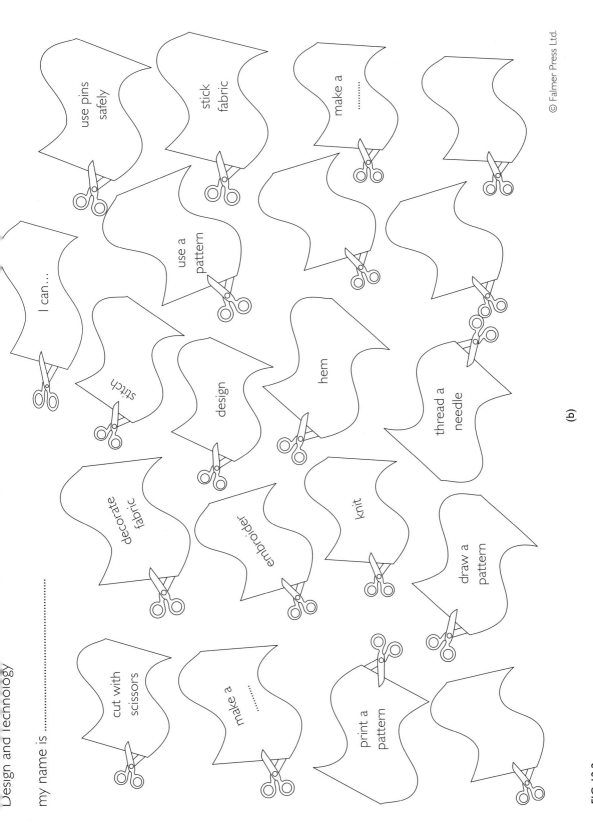

(b)

FIG 12.2
Examples of I can . . . proformas

157

My Design and Technology Plan

I will make a	I will use these materials

I will use these tools

It will look like this

FIG 12.3a
Example of a 'design and make' planning proforma which might be used with infants

Design and Technology — Planning

I am working with these friends ....

We have decided to ...

Our ideas are ...

We want it to ...

We will start by ...

Later we will ...

Then we will ...

When it is finished it will look like this

FIG 12.3b
Example of a 'design and make' planning proforma which might be used with older or more experienced children

is representative of the child's achievement and scope of work. It is likely that the portfolio would include photographs of 3D work and 2D work including, plans, pictures, diagrams and various forms of writing. The school may already have such portfolios or records of achievement and so design and technology should follow and seek to develop current practice. If such things do not exist you will need to consider:

- the purpose of such a record;
- the audience for such a record;
- frequency of samples;
- that all items should be dated;
- that you might include a teacher comment;
- that you might include a child's comment;
- that you might include a parental comment;
- that at the end of the year all or part of the portfolio would be passed on to the next teacher;
- storage and security of the record.

Classroom discussion

Teachers can assess much about their children through discussion. This is often best for assessment when the teacher is prepared to direct and promote the discussion with a light touch. That is, the children take a leading part in the discussion with the teacher listening carefully — listening and questioning may be the two most important skills for the teacher. Because discussions are so expensive in terms of teacher time, the teacher should make use of class, group and individual discussion. The first two can be very efficient at identifying the children that the teacher needs to see individually.

Assess the detail and the holistic view

In design and technology there is detail upon which we can focus as learning objectives and assessment criteria; can the child construct a plan? to what extent does the child consider the characteristics of the material being used? This is necessary and important. It is also important to take a little time to 'step back' and look at the broader picture. Is the child producing a worthwhile product? Does the child see the needs of user or client? It is, therefore, good advice to focus on the detail in relation to your teaching but to take in the wider view of the child's design and technology.

Assessing group work

A complication of design and technology is that teachers often want children to collaborate, but that an inevitable product of this is that it is sometimes difficult to determine who contributed what. This is all the more reason for focusing your assessment on a learning objective and looking for associated evidence. More often than not it will be the role of one or two children which you are unclear about, and questioning will often resolve such issues. The times when you cannot form a judgment will be rare, in which case we ought to be honest and accept it.

Assessing three dimensional work

Where a child has produced a product, be it two or three dimensional you will be assisted in your assessment when you have clear criteria determined at the planning stage about what the learning objective of this session is — what capability are you looking for in the child? In assessing children's work the extent to which children were aware of such criteria is very significant: If you have been designing and making shopping bags and the children have agreed that the criteria for a good shopping bag is to be its carrying strength. Your educational criteria might be to do with the children's craft skills or their ability to work with materials. It is then rather unfair if the teacher then assesses the work against a criteria of neat cutting and lack of glue smudges!

Giving feedback to the children

Where children are self-assessing there ought to be times where they discuss that assessment with their teacher, in order that they get a feel for the accuracy of what they are saying about their achievement. There should be opportunity for this when you give them comments (written and spoken) about both three dimensional and two dimensional work. For many teachers it will feel very natural to give a written comment for two dimensional work but less so for three dimensional work. Could the children design a proforma for comments?

Marking

There may be opportunities to use marking in design and technology. However, we may need to consider the place for marking as perhaps a written dialogue between the teacher and the learner rather than cursory ticks and generalised statements. Oral comments will be made by teachers and children during lessons. Written marking has the advantage of forming a record of your thoughts about the work and requires the child to read a personal comment. Perhaps we ought to be looking in design and technology for carefully chosen comments at particular points in the work? Any school policy documentation on marking should assist here.

Management of assessment for design and technology

Managing assessment and record keeping in the classroom

Assessment may include a combination of so called 'informal assessment', some child self-assessment and more systematic teacher assessment. As design and technology coordinator you need to try different formats of assessment in the classroom, find out as much as you can about it and, importantly, talk in some detail to the teacher in your school responsible for assessment, recording and reporting. Colleagues will need advice about the options available for design and technology.

Will the teacher set aside time in the classroom for assessment?

It is a good idea to be clear in your plan for a day or a lesson when you will make time to talk to children or to observe them working. If you have one or two criteria in mind (based on the lesson objective) make sure that you set a little time aside to focus on assessment. With experience you will use time more efficiently. Often teachers find that they can assess a number of children quite easily, but that a smaller number of children require a little more time to determine their achievement.

Where will I record my assessment?

A simple proforma or notepad with the criteria and a list of the children should allow you to make notes about any absent children or anywhere you need to make a particular comment. Where the activity was broadly suited to the children you will write nothing as they have done as you expected, assuming the lessons objectives have been achieved. Valuable time will be spent considering and noting any children who significantly underachieve or overachieve.

Will assessment be a part of a regular design and technology activity?

As this is teacher assessment it is most appropriate that you assess the children as they work, particularly as your learning objectives will have been carefully chosen to suit the children's needs.

How many children will the teacher assess at one time?

Where the teacher's focus is one or two simple criteria you may be able to assess a number of children in one session, particularly if you know the children well. If you are looking at an aspect of design and technology which is new to you or the children or at several aspects of design and technology, then the assessment will take longer. A child with a developing command of English may need more time as might a child who is a reluctant speaker. The class may divide into three, or four groups which you can focus on for assessment. If you have differentiated in any way for design and technology then those groups may be appropriate for assessment.

How much assessment of design and technology?

Informal assessment might occur on most occasions when design and technology is a significant part of the session. Children's self-assessment may contribute, but you will have to find time for some assessment by yourself. If design and technology is built into two or three half terms in the year you ought to focus on some systematic assessment based on your learning objectives such that you gather some information on the children's achievement in designing and making. The best advice might be to include some assessment in every lesson to the point where you are sufficiently informed to be able to consider seriously the option of differentiation or be able to inform a parent about achievement.

Moderation

As coordinator you can assist teachers in their personal judgments by sharing understanding of the criteria which appear in the levels of the National Curriculum Attainment Targets. The construction of a portfolio of work is a useful focus for this moderation. Short meetings might consider different pieces of 2D and 3D judged against assessment criteria. The important thing is that teachers share their views from the start and that it is accepted from the start that there will be times when you will be unable to agree. Such discussion ought to consider other 'evidence' of achievement, i.e. your conversations with children. Concern or confusion in one area might lead you to an area for development.

End of Key Stage assessment

At the end of each Key Stage (7 and 11 year olds), teachers will be expected to state the level that the child has achieved. This is done by examining a selection of representative work from the child and making a best fit to the Level Descriptor which best describes their achievement to date. The child may not have achieved everything at that level but the level statement chosen should describe the child's achievement better than any other. For end of Key Stage assessment we are advised to avoid breaking the Level Descriptor down into its constituent parts and using each as a criteria, as the system is one of best fit. Initially it may be useful for teachers to select a range of three, four or five children from the class, do some fairly detailed analysis of their work and talk to them to confirm a judgment. This might be followed up by some discussion with colleagues (moderation) about levels. Following these activities the teacher may be more confident to assign other children to levels. It may be more helpful to look for the level that the children are working towards, for example, a child whose 'best fit' statement is the one at level 3 is therefore working towards level 4. This language of 'working towards' is far more positive and implies movement. It might discourage the notion that the complexity of a subject like design and technology can be summed up by a score.

Of course, such levels may mean very little to parents who may easily oversimplify the levels and expect children to go up one level per year! (each level was written to represent two years of progress for an average child).

Reception — end of a Key Stage?

The end of the reception year is as significant as the end of a Key Stage. Does your school conduct assessment during the nursery and reception years? How does this relate to assessment at the end of the reception year? Does this relate in any way to design and technology? Make yourself familiar with your school's present policy and the SCAA, 1996 document *Nursery education: desirable outcomes for children's learning.*

> *They explore and select materials and equipment and use skills such as cutting, joining, folding and building for a variety of purposes.* (SCAA, 1996, p. 12)

Informing parents

As design and technology coordinator you should be concerned about parents' perceptions of the subject and the achievement of children at your school. Parents are usually interested and delighted to see the things that their children have made in school. As they themselves may not have studied design and technology their understanding of the subject and why it is taught may be limited. Like a lot of adults they may group a number of subjects together under the heading 'technology' — they may not, however, consider that work with food is part of technology.

As design and technology coordinator, parents can help you considerably. Their most regular direct contribution has in the past been in the collection of recycled materials for boxcraft and assistance in the classroom. If parents value a subject they will often assist further and support the school in all sorts of ways to further this part of their child's education. In order to value a subject they need to know about it and that it is benefiting their child.

Open events can help to inform parents about what is going on. Parents appreciate the opportunity to have a good look at a range of children's design and technology work and, even better, observe and participate with children working or have a go themselves. This means that they are more likely to value what is happening and to understand what you say about the child's achievement and progress.

Report writing

Parents are likely to have heard from their child about making things at school and it may be that some products have arrived (intact) at home. The annual report is an opportunity to inform parents about their child's achievement and progress in design and technology and thereby inform them about the subject. As coordinator you might like to offer colleagues advice in writing reports. Such advice might refer to possible comments which might include reference to the child's:

- attitude;
- designing;
- making;
- creativity;
- evaluating;
- products;
- the range of the work;
- developing skills;
- developing accuracy;
- creativity;
- ability to cooperate;
- willingness to talk about their work.

You might mention a particular topic or product that the child has designed and made and probably include a final sentence which mentions your expectations for the child in the future: '. . . will need to work carefully and with more accuracy in the future.' '. . . must try to use tools more carefully, . . . now use these new skills to tackle more challenging problems, . . . needs to work hard at focusing attention on the most important aspects of each project.' Your own learning objectives based on the National Curriculum and associated assessment will give you useful references to include.

Try glancing through the report sections you have written, could your words refer to any subject? Is it clear that your comments relate to design and technology?

Parents' evenings

This is a chance for parents to see the range of work in design and technology. Teachers might be encouraged to display work from the children and to make design and technology books, or portfolios, available. Examples of three dimensional work will assist parents greatly in their understanding of what goes on in design and technology.

Newsletters

Newsletters to parents occur in most primary schools and there is an increasing tendency to include in them a curricular content. Why not tell the parents what the children will be doing in design and technology and suggest things that could be done at home to support this work? Chapman (1997) gives a range of practical alternatives.

Conclusion

Assessment, recording and reporting remain a challenge and a great opportunity for design and technology. Teacher assessment encourages teachers to look very hard at the children's achievement against the criteria which are related to learning objectives. Thus attention is drawn to the subject in a way that it otherwise might not be. The other big plus is that teacher assessment provides information. We are getting better as a profession at using information, but at times we still fail to use important information which is right in front of us. If you are monitoring and evaluating design and technology, the results of teacher assessment will be of great interest to you.

Part five   Resources for learning

Chapter 13

Resources for design and technology

Introduction

This chapter will consider the full range of resources that
a primary school might wish to have at its disposal for the
teaching of design and technology. The next chapter goes into
the important question of how these resources are managed
and used. Some people may be of the view that design and
technology in the primary school can be achieved at little
expense. Work out the total annual spending per child and
compare it with the Ofsted figures in the last chapter and
you will see that this is not the case if you want to provide
satisfactory or better teaching. As design and technology
coordinator you must make it clear to senior managers that
good quality design and technology comes at a price. You
must have the purpose of resources clearly in mind.

- To what extent are they needed?
- Which resources are essential?
- Which are desirable?
- Is it the resources which determine the teaching or the
  teaching and learning which leads?

As coordinator you need to build your knowledge about
resources so that as things develop in school you are in a
position to further the achievement of the children through
the correct deployment of the correct resources. There is no
doubt that the resource needs of schools differ widely and

Materials for construction
These will include the following (you might expect that those items marked* may already be available in most classrooms): adhesives* (see below), aluminium foil, balloons, beads, bobbins, boxes* (cardboard), candles, cans (drinks), corks*, correflute, elastic bands* (various), film canisters, foil (metal), garden canes, lollipop sticks, marbles, newspaper*, packaging, paper*, paper fasteners*, paper clips*, pipe insulation, plasticine*, straws*(paper, plastic), strings*, syringes, tapes (sellotape, masking, PVC, parcel), ties (plastic), tubes* (cardboard, plastic), tubing (plastic), wooden dowel, wooden strips, wheels (card, wooden), wire (florists, electrical),

so advice in this chapter must be adapted by you and your colleagues in your school.

There is a danger that this chapter might become a wish list. There will be indication of the characteristics you are looking for in design and technology resources and whether they might be suitable for different age ranges. Some indication will be made as to the minimum that you will need to get by on and what might be considered to be reasonable provision. It may be more realistic to deal with textiles, construction and food one after another as you may have neither the funding nor the energy to do all of them at once. The very important aspects of management of these resources will be dealt with separately in the next chapter along with how resources can contribute to progression.

Resources for design and technology can usefully be considered under the following headings:

- materials for construction including: adhesives, electrical, food, textiles, graphics;
- tools;
- storage;
- teaching areas;
- Information Technology;
- the school site;
- teachers' books and schemes;
- human resources.

You must recognise that you will be a victim of your own success. That is as you gain resources you also gain the considerable task of maintaining and managing those resources.

Materials for construction

While many of these items have to be bought a good number can be collected by the children. If children are not 'good' at bringing things from home it may be possible to train them, perhaps add an element of competition or appeal directly to parents, perhaps through the Parent Teachers Association. You might be sensible to work on the younger children and hope that this engenders a new willingness that will then spread throughout the school. Children need to be constantly collecting some items i.e. cylinders. They need to be responsive, to stop collecting when they are asked and to start collecting when asked. They need to realise that school can only use clean items, that food must not be left in packages, that they should not bring glassware and that they should always avoid items with sharp edges. Try to arrange a drop off point and children to sort items for you.

Adhesives for use in construction

This should be seen as part of the wider knowledge of joining materials. Adhesives are now available in many forms and children need to learn that there is a wide range of adhesives, each having particular properties.

glues	
paste glues	– wallpaper paste, Gloy
paper glues*	– Pritt Sticks, PVA, Marvin, Copydex (some of these will stick textiles)
wood glues*	– wood adhesives, balsa cement
strong glues	– Evo Stick, Bostick (at one time these glues gave off dangerous vapour, most of them have now been re-formulated to avoid this) read instructions carefully, if in doubt do not use
glue guns	– here you should use 'cool' glue guns, this glue is quick to set, safe but a little expensive
epoxy resins	– usually include the glue and a hardener in separate tubes which have to be mixed before they set (this is usually very powerful glue which should be used only when required and under adult supervision)
superglues	– **too dangerous** for use in school as human flesh can be permanently bonded
tapes	
masking tape*	– less messy than other tapes, it is also easy to paint masking tape
Sellotape/Scotch Tape*	– strong and cheap — children are very familiar with it — young children find it 'messy' to use, poor resistance to water — double sided version can be very useful
PVC tape	– comes in various colours, highly waterproof, the adhesive is often not very strong
parcel tape (paper)	– wide — can be painted — needs to be licked!
parcel tape (plastic)	– strong — difficult for young hands — cannot be painted easily — somewhat waterproof when in position
carpet tape (plastic)	– very strong — available in different colours — cannot be painted easily, quite waterproof
(See section on joining in Chapter 4).	

FIG 13.1
Advantages and disadvantages of
construction kits

advantages	disadvantages
■ once purchased, kits are free to use ■ models are quick to build ■ children are often familiar with kits ■ kits in schools can compensate where children do not have them at home ■ kits often contain 'technical' items which can be very difficult to make ■ can speed up experimentation with technical functions, i.e. gears ■ can speed up the modelling process ■ carefully purchased and used, kits can contribute to progression ■ parts fit together easily ■ kits often have activity cards, teachers' books and other support material	■ small parts can be easily lost ■ bricks bear little relation to 'real' materials ■ can attract some children and 'switch-off' others ■ can limit what can be built

Tools for construction

These will include: bench hooks or sawing block (various
designs), mitre blocks, coping saw, drill stand, files, G clamps,
Gents saw, junior hacksaws, tri squares, hammers, hand drill
and bits, hole punch, gimlets, pliers, safety paper cutter,
sandpaper, scissors*, snips and vices.

Construction kits

Construction kits represent a powerful tool for teaching
design and technology in primary education. Owing to their
expense they usually represent a significant investment. Often
purchased without question for children in the early years,
teachers requiring them for older children may need to make
a case for their use. The list of advantages below may assist
and might be included in a school policy.

The progressive use of kits can enable achievement to develop.
You need to experiment with different kits and different age
ranges until you find combinations that are suitable to your
colleagues and children.

Always select construction kits where possible which have:
- suitable teacher support material;
- where support material presents pictures which include positive role models for all children;
- a spares service (or buy a small extra set for spares);
- robust storage (or purchase storage).

When considering kits for an age range think about:
- the range of manipulative skills;
- the children's strength;
- the need to expose them to technical functions and a range of components;
- teacher support materials;
- providing a range for each age group;
- consider mini, midi and maxi versions of the same kit.
(See Figure 14.3 for advice about characteristics of kits for different age ranges.)

Inform your colleagues about:
- the cost of these resources;
- ideas for using kits in the classroom.

Discuss with your colleagues:
- caring for construction kits;
- ways of organising construction kits;
- ways of storing construction kits;
- dealing with negative reactions from individuals and groups;
- assuming that all children know what to do with these kits;
- introducing a new kit to a group of children.

Using kits in the classroom
You must avoid any idea that construction kits are only to be used in free play or, even worse, there to entertain children during wet playtimes (avoid this at all costs). Alternative approaches include using kits to:
- model ideas;
- build prototypes;
- model mechanisms i.e. a hinge or a pulley system;
- set challenges;
- set broad contexts for building;
- for cooperative construction;
- use the workcards provided;

■ make your own workcards;

■ tell a story.

Electrical tools and components for construction

As children progress in their construction they should be encouraged to include simple electrical circuits, switches etc. It is worth discussing with your science coordinator (who may be you!) when it is that children will be introduced to different electrical components in science. This might be followed up by application of the components in design and technology. There may be the possibility of joint purchase of resources.

Resources for food technology

As a somewhat underdeveloped area of design and technology this often requires considerable effort to ensure that it is approached in a professional manner. This is one reason why it was suggested earlier that areas like food and textiles be tackled at different times by the school and the coordinator. Better to delay implementation by a few months, plan well and deal with the area thoroughly.

The highest priority is hygiene. It is safest to assume that neither teachers nor children are knowledgable or equipped to work hygienically. Teachers must understand that they should aspire to the highest possible standards of hygiene. For example cleaning materials (i.e. cloths etc.) used in food technology must be a separate stock. Headteachers need to realise that if this activity is to take place, certain resources are essential and without these, food technology should not be carried out.

The following resources, coupled with suitable routines (see the next chapter), will allow safe and productive food technology:

> antiseptic cleaning agent (i.e. Dettox), aprons, baking tins, baking trays, books* (hygiene, health, other cultures and recipes), cleaning cloths, cutlery and utensils, cutting boards (plastic (separate for meat and other food)), crockery (plastic), detergent, food, grater (rotary), jugs (measuring), juice extractor, knives (various), measuring spoons, mixing bowls, pastry cutters, paper towels, peeler (left and right handed), refrigeration, rolling pins, tea towels, tin opener, scales, scouring pad, sieves, soap, surface cleaner, table cloths (paper or plastic), timer, tin opener, whisk.

Aprons are often a challenging issue as we must have aprons to protect children's clothing and yet dirty aprons are themselves unhygienic: disposable aprons are one option, PVC ones (while expensive) do wipe clean, cotton aprons need washing after use, as do adapted shirts. Whichever option you chose you must establish routines which mean that aprons are only used once and that they are thoroughly cleaned. It is not acceptable to use the aprons which are also used for art. Children have to be aware of the difference and the issue. Aprons might need to be colour coded and should be stored separately.

Heating and cooling facilities

Every design and technology coordinator needs to look carefully at the needs of the school in terms of how teachers can heat and cool food. This might be the subject of a separate audit when you come to the time when you deal with this. The five options in Figure 13.2 all have advantages and disadvantages.

FIG 13.2
Heat sources available for the classroom

form	advantages	disadvantages
electrical cooker	■ children are familiar ■ can heat a lot of food at one go ■ even temperature around oven ■ expensive	■ fixed in a kitchen base area ■ requires supervision (an extra adult)
mini electrical cooker	■ cheaper than other options ■ portable (with care)	■ temperature can vary within over (fan assisted versions better) ■ portability can cause hazards (can be overcome)
electric ring	■ cheap ■ two-ring version available ■ very portable ■ easy to clean	■ portability can cause hazards (can be overcome) ■ limited function
microwave	■ children are increasingly familiar ■ hot food is shut inside ■ timing function clear ■ IT application — cooks quickly	■ food coming out can be very hot ■ not suitable for all food ■ teachers may require training
kettle	■ cheap ■ portable ■ familiar	■ dangerous ■ limited to heating water

Most schools need a mix of these to allow every class access to heating food. Don't forget that it is possible to find practical food based activity which does not require heating (see Chapter 5 on pedagogy and the issue of supervision).

Classes ought to have access to refrigerated storage, but school kitchens may not be allowed to give you access to their facilities. You may have to use a refrigerator in the staff room. Whichever refrigerator you use, you must ensure that there is a routine for keeping it clean and free from waste food.

Food storage

This is an important issue in food technology. As coordinator you need to establish guidelines and routines which will mean that food does not become a hazard. Three areas need to be dealt with:

1   food storage which might lead to infestation;
2   food storage which might lead to food contamination or food going off;
3   food disposal.

Teachers and children (as is relevant to their age) need to understand that:

- Food should never be stored in school for more than a few days, if in doubt throw it away and buy fresh.
- Food should be stored in sealed, waterproof (plastic, rigid) containers.
- Clear labelling of containers is needed.
- Spilt food should always be cleaned up thoroughly.
- Access to any stored food should be restricted to avoid children contaminating food (for example at playtime).
- Fresh food should be refrigerated.

Mobile trolleys for food technology are favoured by many in primary education who are looking for a simple and efficient solution to the resourcing issue. There is no doubt that trolleys have a lot to offer and should be considered. There is further discussion of the potential contribution that they can make to design and technology generally in the next section.

Resources for textiles technology

Sheet textiles

These would include: binka, cotton, felt, hessian, interfacing, lace, press studs, stuffing. Because of cost you might have to limit much of these to off-cuts (see next chapter).

Joining textiles

Textiles can be joined by young children in a variety of ways, some of the following ought to be available: buttons, fabric glue, hooks and eyes, threads, velcro, wonder web, zips.

Decorating textiles

Much primary textiles work can come from children decorating textiles, possibly using: beads, dyes, dye pens, embroidery threads, laces, fabric crayons, fabric pens, feathers, paint on dyes, ribbons, sequins, threads, yarns, wadding.

Tools for textiles technology

These will include:

> carding brushes, chalk, iron (see safety), knitting needles, scissors (good quality), needles (various), needle threader, peg looms, pinking shears, pins, spinning stick, thimbles, unpicking tool, sewing machine (cheap effective ones are available for around £40, see catalogues from suppliers in appendix A), weaving frames and weaving cards printing equipment.

Tool trolleys

Specially designed and in some cases stocked, trolleys can be purchased for construction, food and textiles technology. These have distinct advantages and one or two drawbacks: the biggest drawback is their cost; the second is their inability to negotiate stairs. They also take up a considerable space when not in use, but will often tuck underneath a table. For many schools they have been a helpful addition to the school's design and technology resources. Advantages include: tidiness;

that they provide an extra work surface; that they carry a considerable stock; that re-stocking them is a routine task which can be carried out by children and that they form a considerable focus for design and technology.

Toolboards

These flat wooden boards have a basic set of tools for construction, food or textile technology and they are cheaper and more portable than the trolleys. They tend not to store materials, but do organise your tools for you, providing an 'at a glance' check and like the trolleys make a focus for design and technology. They can stand on a surface, but as such surfaces are at such a premium in primary classrooms may be better hung on the wall.

Quantities of tools required

This is difficult to answer, but important for the design and technology coordinator to consider. First, you need a picture of how much design and technology will be occurring in the next year or two. Then you need to know what sort of technology this will be. This will be much easier if you have a clear curriculum plan. The balance within the technology will be important (i.e. of the hours available how much will be construction?) as will be knowing when it is to occur — will food technology occur in three classes at the same time? The final variable here is teaching style. There is a considerable difference between three classes doing technology, one group at a time or the whole class at a time. This affects curriculum planning as it is desirable to avoid too much overlap. The next chapter will say much about storage of tools, but here we consider numbers.

A very rough guide might consider a one form entry primary school with a nursery, involving eight classes (around 256 children), each doing construction two or three times a year. The school is likely to need three or four class sets of construction tools. The size of a class set is determined by the style of teaching — if a whole class is to use saws at the same time you might need sets of 30+ saws and bench hooks. Alternatively, you might accept that children might share saws and so reduce the numbers to 15+. The bench hooks are useful in many respects as they can be used to protect the table when gluing, hammering and drilling. The need for tools like hand drills or files is less and you might feel that for a whole-class lesson where children physically sit in groups that four, five or six children might then share one or two drills, for example: a class set might include 15+ saws, 15+ bench hooks, 8 G clamps, 8 hand drills and bits and 8 files. Where the teacher is going to organise this activity amongst a group, obviously a smaller set of equipment will be needed — perhaps 6 saws, 6 bench hooks, 6 G clamps, 3 hand drills, 3 files. Beware trying to persuade teachers to change their classroom organisation to save the school a few hundred pounds on resources. Teachers who have difficulty with this subject often find that it is classroom organisation issues which get in the way so it may be better to spend a little more and give teachers a greater chance of success. Senior management needs to be aware of this issue.

In other areas, for example food and textile technology, the position is different. First, you may be doing this less often and second, there may be more variation in whether these aspects are dealt with as a whole class or as a group. For example, simple card weaving is fairly cheap and straightforward to introduce to a class. However, food preparation with one mini cooker is likely for a number of reasons (including the size of the oven and the level of supervision required) to be a group activity in the primary setting (see next chapter).

Specialised rooms/areas

Schools with the space have provided a technology room where all the resources have been stored and where classes can go on a rota basis. There are examples where this has worked, but it has often been aided by the provision, in some way, of an extra adult to help manage or use the room. These adults have been classroom assistants, parents, technicians and on other occasions, the headteacher.

This idea has advantages, perhaps the greatest of which is the focus of resources and activity in one place. The biggest disadvantage is to do with supervision and the fact that this area is separate from the classroom which goes against some of the advantages of the subject as a cross-curricular vehicle.

The most common specialised area used in technology is a kitchen area. This has obvious advantages as children are very familiar with kitchens. It helps to avoid some of the hygiene problems in the classrooms and reinforces messages directly about work habits in kitchens. Supervision of groups is a challenge for many schools, as is finding first the space and then the funding for such an area.

General teaching areas

Most primary design and technology is taught in generalist teaching areas. Usually extra resources are brought in and these are often well organised. Thought needs to be given to where design and technology takes place. The space should:
■ be sufficient in terms of workbench area and floorspace;
■ be away from main thoroughfares;
■ be adjacent to relevant resources;
■ allow sufficient supervision for the activity;
■ be well lit.

Where possible such areas should contain well organised and presented tools, books, artefacts etc. which promote an atmosphere of organisation and quality. Primary teachers are used to creating a stimulating environment, they may be less used to including displays of or about design and technology.

Teaching resources for teachers

There is an increasing availability of books and other material that teachers can use for ideas and guidance. These are often good on ideas and general advice and less detailed on aspects like differentiation and progression. Teachers need at their disposal a range of materials which will allow them to develop the themes that they are allocated and teach the skills and knowledge required.

While many of the issues below will be mentioned in your school policy the nature of the policy will necessitate brevity. You are looking for a bank of resources which you might build up to provide more detail and background on:

- ideas for approaches to your chosen themes;
- advice about organisation and classroom management;
- advice about use of tools;
- advice about safety.

You should make it clear to teachers through your action and policy documentation for design and technology that support is available. You should make the nature of the support and its location clear. Whilst some teachers will perhaps need the security of a published scheme, at least for a while. Others will find such a scheme constraining. As coordinator you ought to recognise that the teachers are your greatest resource and that written resources are simply important tools for you in your role of enabling teachers and children to achieve excellent results.

Information Technology

The full potential for Information Technology as a resource in design and technology has not yet been established in many primary schools. This may be a significant area for development but may require the purchase of software. Several IT themes can easily be developed through design and technology (see Figure 13.3).

FIG 13.3
Opportunity for IT in design and technology (for suppliers' details see Appendix A)

IT theme	design and technology (example)	software (example)
communication	<ul><li>writing</li><li>drawing</li></ul>	<ul><li>Pages (SEMERC)</li><li>Splosh (Kudlian)</li></ul>
design/modelling	<ul><li>drawing</li><li>design a bedroom</li></ul>	<ul><li>Computer Aided Design (SEMERC)</li><li>3D Bedroom Designer (SEMERC)</li></ul>
control	<ul><li>controlling a door</li><li>controlling a buggy</li><li>programmable toy</li></ul>	<ul><li>Co-Co (Commotion)</li><li>Contact (NCET)</li><li>Roamer (Valiant Technology)</li></ul>
application	<ul><li>design and technology in the world</li></ul>	<ul><li>Technology and Design CD ROM (SEMERC)</li></ul>
data handling	<ul><li>comparing materials</li></ul>	<ul><li>Datasweet (Kudlian)</li></ul>

The environment as a resource for design and technology

The whole environment is undoubtedly a resource for design and technology as part of primary education. Within the whole environment we can identify localised environments that can be used by teachers of design and technology. A major advantage of these is that children will be familiar with them and the associated vocabulary.

The local community

The local community and area will include buildings, bridges, parks, play areas, pathways and roads, materials, surfaces, workplaces and homes, all of which provide a context in which we can identify needs, and to seek to provide plans and products which will fulfil those needs.

The school

The school building and its grounds will provide extensive opportunities to deal with needs associated with safety, use of resources, signs, pollution, storage and work.

Environmental awareness

The environment was identified by the National Curriculum Council in 1990 as a cross-curricular theme (NCC, 1990). This is certainly an area which interests children. The NCC identified three aspects of this environmental education.

FIG 13.4
Three aspects of environmental education (based on NCC, 1990)

Three aspects of environmental education	Examples from design and technology
education in the environment	children visit a part of the school grounds to gather information, prior to then designing an outside classroom
education about the environment	children learn about the characteristics of plants and their suitability for this project
education for the environment	children design a litter prevention policy for the area

As can be seen, this can easily tie in with topic initiatives in school.

Staffing

Teachers

The most important resource, people, has been left to the last in this section. It is essential that teachers are enabled to teach the subject effectively. That means good organisation, by you as coordinator, good resourcing and good training. All of this will not guarantee good design and technology achievement but will make it possible. It is therefore essential that you gather evidence so that you can monitor and evaluate and thereby ensure that future funding is well directed.

This will be essential to consider in any audit of the subject. How do the staff feel? What are the areas they are concerned about? What expertise is available in the school?

Adult assistance in the classroom

This may come in the form of classroom assistants, nursery nurses, parents or students doing placements or teaching practice in school. Such adults are likely to be of great assistance to teachers dealing with design and technology. Teachers should be encouraged to view extra support positively. They should be asked to inform these adults about the level of supervision required, any safety issues, the fact that we want the children to do as much as possible for themselves and what the objectives of the activity are. You might consider some kind of training for parent helpers.

Non teaching school staff

As children's work in design and technology will mean that they are interested in problems faced within school: moving heavy loads around, materials, hygiene etc. Teachers are likely to ask children to talk to those working in school, so you should make the opportunity to prepare non-teaching colleagues so that they know what to expect.

Conclusion

For many design and technology coordinators this chapter will be a focus of much attention and can give a feeling of achievement early on. It is possible to resource a school well if funds can be found. What is far more important is what is done with the resources. It may be better to build them up more slowly and tie in staff development so that you can be more certain that they will be used to good effect. Then, when you argue for resources in the future you will be able to show that money spent on design and technology is well spent.

Chapter 14

Managing resources

Introduction

The management of resources for design and technology should aim to ensure that resources contribute in every way possible to the children's achievement in design and technology. As the coordinator, your management of these resources is as important as the resources themselves. It is suggested that the coordinator formulates a resource map (Figure 14.1) and includes specific reference to resources in the subject action plan:

■ what do we have now?;
■ where do we want to be? and;
■ how and when will we get there?.

As choosing and using resources is an important capability in young children, you could involve them in choosing, storing and organising the resources. A spin off from such an approach is less day to day work for yourself and colleagues.

Whole-school management of design and technology resources

There are a number of aspects to management at the school level. The objective is to ensure **sufficient** of the **right resources** in the **right place** at the **right time**. This could be solved by a huge budget which would supply each class with everything that they might need. In reality a primary school needs to make the best provision with limited resources. This again matches what design and technologists do in the real world, they have an idea of the standard or quality to which they aspire and then they seek to design and plan a product which will achieve this within the resources available. Schools need to provide certain resources in classrooms (many are already there, see the items marked with a * in Chapter 13) which might mean a technology resource in each room (see below) and sufficient central resources to supply particular themes as required.

Most typically, design and technology resources are stored in a central area. Such a central resource must provide for construction, textile and food technology and needs some attention to ensure that the right balance is achieved. The curriculum plan which includes design and technology will also provide a tool itself to ensure resources are spread evenly. One measure of a well-managed central resource would be that it might be empty for large parts of the year!

We have already suggested an audit of design and technology. An audit of school resources ought to feature as part of this early on, as you will need to have a clear picture of what is available before you put in a bid for funds.

A whole-school design and technology resource map

Such a plan will set out what you hope to establish and might be part of your medium term plan. Large capital items like trolleys and cookers may be paid for out of another school fund additional to your design and technology budget.

A resource plan (Figure 14.1) describes the situation in a number of schools and it may be that by considering this you can see an alternative which suits your school.

The detail of this plan is not important. The important points are that:
■ all resources are considered;
■ some resources are seen to be age range specific (i.e. different construction kits for different age ranges), extension of this

FIG 14.1
A whole-school resource map for
design and technology

classes	N	R	Yr 1	Yr 2	Yr 3	Yr 4	Yr 5	Yr 6
each class has a class design and technology resource	early year class resources				later primary class resources			
			middle primary class resources					
construction kits	nursery/reception set		year 1 set	year 2 set	year 3 set	year 4 set	year 5 set	year 6 set
construction tools	a main infant/early years resource serves N–Yr 2				a main junior resource serves years 3–6			
food technology	nursery & reception have their own stock (including mini-cooker and fridge)				a main resource serves years 1–6 (one food trolley available) two microwaves on trolleys available			
fabric technology	a main resource serves the whole school (two fabric tool boards available)							

will be suggested later as it is a powerful mechanism for
evidencing progression;

- some resource bases are whole-school resource bases (fabric);
- some resource bases are phase specific (construction tools);
- some recognition that special requirements exist (nursery
  and reception have their own stock of food technology
  equipment).

Individual classbase design and technology resources

This might be a specially provided box containing a small set
of construction tools and stitchcraft resources. The examples
in Figure 14.2 shows how you might suggest progression in
your resource provision and assumes that classes are
reasonably resourced with 'basics'.

The class resources would need to tie in with your plans for
progression (see Chapter 6). Where there is a child with specific
needs you might supply a particular piece of equipment — a
saw with a larger handle or clamps, to hold work still. These
resource boxes might be of a particular colour (colour coded)

FIG 14.2
Class based resource boxes

An early years class resource box	A middle years class resource box	A later primary years resource box
■ several pairs of good scissors ■ a junior hacksaw and vice ■ a hammer and nails ■ a roll of masking tape	■ several pairs of good scissors or snips ■ a tape measure ■ a junior hacksaw ■ a small vice ■ sandpaper ■ a roll of masking tape ■ a roll of PVC tape ■ a (cool) glue gun ■ some electrical items — wire, bulbs, bulb holders, a battery ■ a small selection of wood — strip and dowel ■ a small stitchcraft set — needles, pins, felt squares, thimble ■ a hole punch	■ several pairs of good scissors ■ snips ■ pliers ■ a metal tape measure ■ a junior hacksaw ■ a small vice ■ sandpaper ■ a bench hook ■ a roll of masking tape ■ a roll of PVC tape ■ a (cool) glue gun ■ some electrical items — wire, bulbs, bulb holders, a battery ■ a small selection of wood — strip and dowel ■ a small stitchcraft set — needles, pins, felt squares, thimble ■ paper cutting tools

with a neat label saying what is contained. This will allow the class to look after the resources and you to involve other, perhaps older children, to collect the boxes in each half term, check contents and return them. The children might also be responsible for maintaining the lists of contents on a computer spreadsheet. The job of the coordinator might be seen as one who manages rather than one who does everything personally. (You might offer a prize to classes who take care of resources — assuming that they are using them!).

Construction kits

Rather than give brand names Figure 14.3 provides some of the characteristics we should look for and which should promote progression. In each class you are wanting to provide for play opportunities where less mature children can 'catch-up' and where able children can extend. This plan for construction kits

FIG 14.3
A school plan for construction kits

nursery reception	■ pile and stack bricks etc. ■ press to fix sets ■ push to click sets ■ large nuts, bolts and gear wheel sets ■ ride on (maxi) kits ■ large, visual, simple instruction cards ■ large gear sets
year 1	■ push and click basic sets, a variety of wheels ■ press to fix sets ■ nuts, bolts and gear sets ■ medium and maxi sets ■ large visual, simple instruction cards
year 2	■ push and click sets, more technical functions ■ variety in wheels, gears etc. ■ large visual and simple step by step instruction cards ■ mini and medium sets (separate infant and junior schools should liaise here)
year 3	■ push to click sets ■ slot to fit sets ■ a good range of technical functions ■ simple motorisation including switches ■ a range of instruction cards
year 4	■ push to click sets ■ slot to fit sets ■ a good range of technical functions, electrical and simple pneumatics ■ simple motorisation ■ a range of instruction cards
years 5	■ push to click sets ■ slot to fit sets ■ motorisation ■ a wide range of technical and electronic functions ■ sets which include computer control
year 6	■ push to click sets ■ slot to fit sets ■ motorisation ■ a wide range of technical and electronic functions ■ sets which include computer control or pneumatics (liaison with the high school might be useful here)

means that sets of kits would exist for different year groups and it assumes that older juniors benefit from having construction kits available. This is rarely doubted by teachers of primary design and technology but sometimes parents and even headteachers need convincing that their use is educational. Where you have two classes in a year or department, different construction kits might rotate around these classes. Such rotation is worth considering for example around Key Stage 1. A useful basis is the idea that you give children items to play with one year which they will use to build with some time later. You will be able to assume some familiarity with electric motors in Year 4 if you know that such items have featured in play with construction kits earlier on.

In order to make the most of what you have you may be able to buy spares cheaply which would add technical functions (gears, axles, wheels, motors) to existing sets which contain only basic bricks. Where spares are not available you might purchase an extra set of the kit and use it for spares. If your school holds a toy fair, where children bring and buy old toys, you might arrange that the school buys any construction kits in good condition.

A whole-school resource

Textiles

In Figure 14.1 it was suggested that such a resource was established for textiles technology. It may be that you physically split it within the building so that teachers avoid walking up four flights of stairs, or in splitting the resources you differentiate in order to produce an infant resource and a junior resource. Whichever, you will need a substantial base: a sizeable cupboard, store room or set of shelves. Shelving is often in short supply, so an alternative could be sufficient, strong storage boxes which need to be accessible, labelled and clean. You may need to allocate some of your spending to storage.

It is unlikely that you will find a store big enough for construction, food and textiles in one area, therefore it will be necessary to establish several central stores around school. You might consider combining with the art coordinator on a joint textiles store, even if you have a separate stock.

If possible, provide tool boxes or trays for teachers to select their own sets of tools and take them away, thus leaving some stock and storage boxes behind. As an alternative make up a series of boxes or, for example, toolboards which include particular items and are taken away as a unit. There are advantages and disadvantages for you and the teacher in terms of storage. It is worth talking to staff prior to purchasing items like toolboards etc. to get the teachers' views and to give them a sense of commitment to the system which is ultimately implemented.

Food technology resources

Here you need specific stores and systems to ensure that the equipment is hygienic, some advice has been given in Chapter 13. I suggest that you read a book like *Working With Food in Primary Schools* by Jenny Ridgewell (ISBN 0 95 21645 2 3) and to make such books available to colleagues (See Appendix B — Useful Publications). Specific advice should be included in your policy or in an appendix to it. A number of teachers find practical food preparation impossibly difficult, so your job as coordinator is to take a number of simple steps to make it possible.

Considerations for your central food resource:
■ how much equipment is required?
■ how will cleaning materials be provided (sets available in this resource?)?
■ how can we ensure that equipment is put away clean and dry?
■ how will we ensure that damaged equipment is reported?
■ food items must not be stored;
■ equipment should be thoroughly cleaned prior to and following use by a class;
■ equipment should be clearly labelled as stock for school food technology;
■ you should have a central stock of cleaning materials.

Bidding for resources
This is routine in some schools and is used by headteachers for a variety of reasons. If your school operates a bidding system it may be that you are only required to provide a list of items required. Information you can provide as to why a resource is required and how it will be used will inform those who determine which bids are successful. It is often a good idea to distinguish between those things which are essential to continue what you are doing or those needed to fulfil statutory requirements and resources which will allow new developments. Whether your school has a formal system or not, it is worth prioritising and having resources within your subject action plan. You need to be prepared so that when money becomes available you are ready to offer a bid at short notice. Bids are always assisted by a short (often very short) written statement which explains the positive effect of this resource — why the school needs this resource, exactly who will use it, how it will contribute to what you already have or enable things which cannot presently be done in school, state how children will benefit. It is helpful if you can quote an example of a school who is using it successfully or an occasion when you might have used it. You should provide a costing and consider related costs of storage boxes etc. and implications like training.

Consider some evaluation of resources prior to spending. You may be able to loan or purchase a small quantity to evaluate with children.

Short term food storage

Teachers may need to store food in their classrooms, perhaps overnight even, and, of course, certain foods will require refrigeration. They should be encouraged to store food for a minimum amount of time in school and never to store food for more than a few days. Food stored in classrooms should always be in sealed containers, and placed in a secure place so that children cannot remove or add items undetected and so that vermin cannot get access.

Food stored in refrigerators also should be sealed in boxes, and carefully labelled, or you may find the staff have 'borrowed' it or eaten it!

Children taking food home

Children and parents need to be aware in advance that children will be taking food home and need to be aware of the sort of container required. A clean plastic food container with a sealed lid is ideal and can be easily carried in a plastic or paper carrier bag. Children should never be asked by school to carry glass containers of any description.

Heating food

Various options were examined in Chapter 13 and an example of a whole school plan was given earlier in this chapter. Teachers need good advice about heating food, the use of the equipment and the kind of supervision required. And trolleys you use should have large, secure wheels, at least two of which are locking. Equipment which is to be used for heating food in school should be housed carefully and supervised closely. Children should never have unsupervised access to heating devices.

Classroom management of resources

Schools need to consider carefully the advice given to teachers and the degree to which it removes teacher autonomy. For example we might say to teachers that all classrooms must have a permanent design and technology resource. Many

Finding a Space

This is a problem for teachers as they are regularly told what to include in their classrooms but never what to get rid of. It is a good idea periodically to look at each piece of furniture and ask why it is included in the classroom. The teacher's desk is a good example: what purpose does it serve? is there an alternative? We often keep items of furniture because they have always been there. Can storage for some items be found elsewhere? Are there new forms of storage that would create space in the room?

Parents paying for design and technology

You need a school policy on this and will need to talk to colleagues, the headteacher and ideally to parents. Parents are most often asked to contribute to food technology. Any contribution made by parents can only be voluntary. Will children be asked to contribute food or money? Money is in many cases preferred as it means that you are in control of the food, its type, source, purchase and storage. However, many teachers appreciate that some homes will find cash contributions problematic. It may be better to ask for a small sum and be successful than ask for more and have problems. Schools are often happy to subsidise part or all of the cost of reasonable items.

Why not ask the parents what they think about this? What do they think is reasonable?

teachers would be only too happy to go along with your plans, so try to involve them in decisions then they can feel they have ownership.

This book assumes that all classrooms need a permanent home for a small collection of design and technology resources but that this small collection will need to grow at times when it is the class's turn to have a major focus on textiles.

Finding space

Design and technology resources can be easily combined with science or art resources. For some parts of the year you will need perhaps only a shelf, at other times you will need more flat surfaces for the storage and access of materials and tools.

Storage of resources in the classroom

Investment in a variety of storage boxes will assist greatly. See-through plastic toffee jars are excellent for storing matchsticks and other small items. Resources should be clearly labelled and you might have posters close by (perhaps drawn by the children), offering advice about care of and use of tools or safety measures.

Children accessing tools

You should negotiate an access regime for design and technology tools and materials. Some children are responsible and can accept and keep to sensible rules. Other children have difficulty with such constraints. Perhaps such learning is as important for these children as the statutory requirements of the subject?

It is generally good practice to expect children to get their own resources out, though teachers often 'put out' the basics to speed things up, but they need to be aware of what they are doing if they always get out the tools and materials and thus restrict access.

A useful idea is to provide children doing design and technology with a small but empty toolbox which they stock during the lesson. This means that they will know where their tools are and they will be able to carry several tools around the room safely. It also means that you do not have the burden of putting out tools prior to the lesson.

Training implications

We should never assume that colleagues know how to get the best out of a resource and should consider seriously the need for training in areas of design and technology which relate to resources: cutting tools and their correct use, construction kits, information technology. Training events do not have to be whole days, they can be 15 minutes or half hour slots in other meetings.

Conclusion

For many of your teacher colleagues your managing of the school's design and technology resources will be a measure of your success as coordinator. You will never have everything that everyone wants, but if you can show that you are engaged with the task of providing them with good support materials they will appreciate your efforts. The bottom line remains the children's achievement. Resources can certainly affect the breadth of achievement. Once you have the resources, maintaining and improving achievement is harder to achieve, but staff training is one sure way to see improvement.

Useful addresses

Commotion Ltd
Unit 11
Tannery Road
Tonbridge
Kent TN9 1RF
tel. 01732 773399
fax. 01732 773390

DATA (The Design and Technology Association)
16 Wellesbourne House
Walton Road
Wellesbourne
Warwickshire CV35 9JB
tel. 01789 470007
fax. 01789 841955
Email. Data@dandt.demon.co.uk
Internet see NCET site

Economatics Education Ltd
Epic House
Darnell Road
Attercliffe
Sheffield S9 5AA
tel. 01142 813344
fax. 01142 439306

Data Harvest Group
Educational Electronics Ltd
Woburn Road
Waterloo Lodge
Leighton Buzzard
Bedfordshire
LU7 7NR
tel. 01525 373666
fax. 01525 851638
Email. sales@dharvest.demon.co.uk

Heron Educational Ltd
Carrwood House
Carrwood Road
Chesterfield S41 9QB
tel. 01246 453354
fax. 01246 260876
http://www.heron-educational.co.uk

JPR Electronics
Unit M
Kingsway Industrial Estate
Kingsway
Luton
Bedfordshire LU1 1LP
tel. 01582 410055

Kudlian Soft
8 Barrow Road
Kenilworth
Warwickshire
CV8 1EH
tel. 01926 842544
fax. 01926 843537
Email. sales@kudlian.demon.co.uk

Lego (UK) Ltd
Ruthin Road
Wrexham
Clwyd LL13 7TQ
tel. 01978 290900
fax. 01978 296239

Email. legodactauk@aol.com
Internet http://www.lego.com

Logotron Ltd
124 Cambridge Science Park
Milton Road
Cambridge
CB4 2ZS
tel. 01223 425558
fax. 01223 425349
Email. info@logo.com
Internet http://www.logo.com

National Association of Advisers and Inspectors of Design
and Technology
124 Kidmore Road
Caversham
Reading
RG4 7NB
(Publications available from DATA)

National Association of Teachers of Home Economics and
Technology
Hamilton House
Mabledon Place
London WC1 H 9BJ
tel. 0171 387 1441
fax. 0171 383 7230

NCET
Sir William Lyons Road
Science Park
Coventry CV4 7EZ
tel. 01203 416994
fax. 01203 411418
Internet http://www.ncet.org.uk

North West SEMERC
1 Broadbent Road
Watersheddings
Oldham
Ol1 4LB

tel. 0161 627 4469
fax. 0161 627 2381
Email. info@semerc.demon.co.uk

Surplus Buying Agency
Southfield CPD Centre
Gleadless Road
Sheffield S12 2QB
tel. 0114 2646186

Technology Teaching Systems
Unit 7
Monk Road
Alfreton
Derbyshire
DE55 7RL
tel. 01773 830255
fax. 01773 830325
Email. sales@tts/grp.co.uk
Internet http://www.tts/grp.co.uk

Trylon Ltd
Thrift Street
Wollaston
Northamptonshire NN9 7QJ
tel. 01933 664275
fax. 01933 664960

Wirral LEA
Wirral Professional Development Centre
Acre Lane
Bromborough
Wirral
L62 7BZ
tel. 0151 346 1182

Woodcrafty
Craft Products
Ivy House
Deep Cutting
Pool Quay
Welshpool

Powys
SY21 9LJ
tel. 01938 590533

Yorkshire Purchasing Organisation
41 Industrial Park
Wakefield WF2 0XE
tel. 01924 824477
fax. 01924 834805

Appendix B   Useful publications

ALLEN, A. (1989), *The Usbourne Guide to Sewing and Knitting* (London: Usbourne) ISBN 07460 0413 3

BINDON, A. and COLE, P. (1992), *Teaching Design and Technology in the Primary Classroom* (London: Blackie)

BOYLE, D., PITT, W. and TILL, W. (1992), *S.T.E.P: Design and Technology 5–16 Datafile: Key Stage 2* (Cambridge: Cambridge University Press)

DESIGN AND TECHNOLOGY ASSOCIATION (1995), *Guidance Material for Design and Technology at Key Stage 1 and 2* (Wellesbourne: DATA)

DESIGN AND TECHNOLOGY ASSOCIATION, *Design and Technology Primary Coordinator's File* (Wellesbourne: DATA)

NATIONAL COUNCIL FOR EDUCATIONAL TECHNOLOGY (1989), *Techniques in Technology* (Chesterfield: Technology Teaching Systems)

NATIONAL CURRICULUM COUNCIL (1993), *Knowledge and Understanding for Teachers* (Energy, York: NCC) ISBN 1 85838 012 X

NATIONAL CURRICULUM COUNCIL (1993), *Knowledge and Understanding for Teachers: Electricity and Magnetism* York: NCC) ISBN 1 872676 97 9

RIDGEWELL, J. and DAVIES, L. (1989), *Skills in Home Economics: Textiles* (London: Heinemann) ISBN 0 435 4200 1

RIDGEWELL, J. (1993), *Tasting and Testing* (London: Ridgewell Press) ISBN 0 9921645 0 7

WIRRAL LEA (1996), *Schemes of Work and Guidance Key Stage 1 and 2: Design and Technology* (Bromborough: Metropolitian Borough of Wirral)

References

AHLBERG, A. and AHLBERG, J. (1980), *Mrs. Wobble the Waitress* (London: Penguin)

AHLBERG, J. and AHLBERG, A. (1977), *Burglar Bill* (London: Heinemann)

ALEXANDER, A., ROSE, J. and WOODHEAD, C. (1992), *Curriculum Organisation and Practice in Primary Schools* (London: DES)

ALEXANDER, R. (1992), *Policy and Practice in Primary Education* (London: Routledge)

ARCHER, B., BAYNES, K. and ROBERTS, P. (1992), *The Nature of Research into Design and Technology* (Loughborough: Loughborough University of Technology)

ASSOCIATION OF SCIENCE EDUCATION (1990), *Be Safe!* (Hatfield: ASE)

ASSOCIATION OF SCIENCE EDUCATION (1991), *Technology — Policy Statement* (Hatfield: ASE)

AUSUBEL, D. (1968), *Educational Psychology* (New York: Holt, Reinhart and Winston)

BAYNES, K. (1992), *Children's Designing — Learning Design: Occasional Paper No 1* (Loughborough: Loughborough University of Technology)

BELL, J. (1987), *Doing Your Research Project* (Buckinghamshire: Open University Press)

BINDON, A. and COLE, P. (1991), *Teaching Design and Technology in the Primary Classroom* (London: Blackie)

BROWNE, N. and ROSS, C. (1991), 'Girls' stuff, boys' stuff young children playing and talking', in BROWN, N. (ed) *Science and Technology in the Early Years* (Milton Keynes: OUP)

CAMPBELL, J. (1994), 'Managing the primary curriculum: The issue of time allocation', *Education 3–13*, **22**, 1, pp. 3–13

CHAPMAN, C. (1997), 'Home–School Links in Science', in CROSS, A. and PEET, G. (eds) *Teaching Science in the Primary School: Book 1* (Plymouth: Northcote House)

CROSS, A. (1994a), *Design and Technology 5 to 11* (London: Hodder and Stoughton)

CROSS, A. (1994b), 'Coordinating design and technology in the primary school', in HARRISON, M. (ed) *Beyond the Core Curriculum* (Plymouth: Northcote House Publishers)

CROSS, A. (1996), 'Comments related to the teaching of design and technology by school inspectors in primary inspection reports', *The Journal of Design and Technology Education*, **1**, 2, Summer pp. 136–140

CROSS, A. and CROSS, S.V. (1994), 'Organising a professional development day for your colleagues', in HARRISON, M. *Beyond the Core Curriculum* (Plymouth: Northcote House)

CROSS, A. and PEET, G. (eds) (forthcoming), *Teaching Science in the Primary School: Book 1* (Plymouth: Northcote House)

CROSS, A. and CHINN, A. (1977), 'Monitoring and evaluating science in the primary school', in CROSS, A. and PEET, G. (eds) *Teaching Science in the Primary School: Book 1* (Plymouth: Northcote House)

CROSS, A. and HARRISON, H. (1995), *Developmental! An evaluation of Manchester's raising standards in inner city school project 1993–1996* (unpublished report) (Department of Education: University of Manchester)

DEARING, R. (1993), *The National Curriculum and its Assessment: Final Report* (London: School Curriculum and Assessment Authority)

DEPARTMENT FOR EDUCATION (1992), *Technology for Ages 5 to 16 (1992)* (London: HMSO)

DEPARTMENT FOR EDUCATION (1995), *Design and Technology in the National Curriculum* (London: HMSO)

DEPARTMENT FOR EDUCATION AND THE WELSH OFFICE (1991), *Technology: Key Stages 1, 2 and 3: A Report by HM Inspectorate on the Second Year, 1990–1* (London: HMSO)

DEPARTMENT FOR EDUCATION AND THE WELSH OFFICE (1992a), *Curriculum organisation and classroom practice: A discussion paper* (London: DES)

DEPARTMENT OF EDUCATION AND SCIENCE (1990a), *Technology in the National Curriculum* (London: HMSO)

DEPARTMENT OF EDUCATION AND SCIENCE (1990b), *Technology in the National Curriculum: Non Statutory Guidance* (London: HMSO)

DESIGN COUNCIL (1987), *Design and Primary Education* (London: The Design Council)

DESIGN COUNCIL (1991), *Stories as Starting Points for Design and Technology* (London: The Design Council)

DEWHURST, J. (1996), 'Differentiation in primary teaching', *Education 3–13*, **24**, 3

DONALDSON, M. (1978), *Children's Minds* (London: Fontana Press)

DRIVER, R. (1983), *The Pupil as Scientist* (Buckingham: Open University Press)

EASON, P. (1985), *Making School Centred INSET Work* (Buckinghamshire: Open University Press)

EGGLESTON, J. (1992), *Teaching Design and Technology* (Milton Keynes: OUP)

HARLEN, W. (1985), *Taking the Plunge* (London: Heinemann)

HARLEN, W. (1992), *The Teaching of Science* (London: David Fulton)

HARLEN, W., DARWIN, A. and MURPHY, M. (1997), *Match and Mismatch: Raising Questions* (Edinburgh: Oliver and Boyd)

HMI (1987), *Craft, Design and Technology from 5 to 16* (London: HMSO)

HMI (1992), *Technology Key Stages 1, 2 and 3: A Report by HM Inspectorate on the First Year 1990–1* (London: HMSO)

HMI (1993), *Technology Key Stages 1, 2 and 3: A Report on the Third Year 1992–3* (London: HMSO)

JARVIS, T. (1993), *Teaching Design and Technology in the Primary School* (London: Routledge)

JOHNSEY, R. (1990), *Design and Technology Through Problem Solving* (London: Simon and Schuster)

KIMBELL, R. (1994), 'Progression in learning and the assessment of children's attainments in technology', *International Journal of Design and Technology*, **4**, 1, pp. 65–83, (Dordrecht: Kluwer)

KIMBELL, R. (1995), 'Uncertain Crossing', *Times Educational Supplement*, 20 October p. ii

KIMBELL, R., STABLES, K. and GREEN, R. (1996), *Understanding Practice in Design and Technology* (Buckingham: Open University Press)

KIMBELL, R., STABLES, K., WHEELER, T., WOZNIAK, A. and KELLY, V. (1991), *The Assessment of Performance in Design and Technology: The Final Report of the Design and Technology APU Project* (London: Evaluation and Monitoring Unit. Schools Examination and Assessment Council (SEAC))

LAYTON, D. (1991), *Aspects of National Curriculum Design and Technology* (York: National Curriculum Council)

LAYTON, D. (1992a), 'Values in Design and Technology', in BUDGETT-MEAKIN, C. (ed) *Make the Future Work: Appropriate Technology a Teachers Guide* (London: Longman)

LAYTON, D. (1992b), *Values in Design and Technology*, Design Curriculum Matters: 2, Department of Design and Technology (Loughborough: Loughborough University of Technology)

LAYTON, D. (1993), *Technology's Challenge to Science Education* (Milton Keynes: OU Press)

LEVER, C. (1990), *National Curriculum Design and Technology for Key Stages 1, 2 and 3* (Stoke-on-Trent: Trentham Books)

LEWIS, A. (1992), 'From planning to practice', *British Journal of Special Education*, **19**, 1, pp. 24–7

LEYLAND, G. (1988), 'Taking the pain out of training', *Questions*, December, pp. 16–17

MCGUIGAN, L. and SCHILLING, M. (1997), 'Children learning in science', in CROSS, A. and PEET, G. (eds) *Teaching Science in the Primary School: Book 1* (Plymouth: Northcote House Publishing)

MCNAMARA, D. (1984), *Classroom Pedagogy and Primary Practice* (London: Routledge)

MAKIYA, H. and ROGERS, M. (1992), *Design and Technology in the Primary School* (London: Routledge)

NATIONAL ASSOCIATION OF ADVISERS AND INSPECTORS OF DESIGN AND TECHNOLOGY (1992), *Make it Safe* (Caversham: NAAIDT)

NATIONAL CURRICULUM COUNCIL (1990), *Curriculum Guidance 7: Environmental Education* (York: National Curriculum Council)

NATIONAL CURRICULUM COUNCIL (1993), *Technology Programmes of Study and Attainment Targets: Recommendations of the NCC* (York: NCC)

NAYLOR, S. and KEOGH, B. (1997), 'Progression in Primary Science', in CROSS. A. and PEET, G. (eds) *Teaching Science in the Primary School Book 1* (Plymouth: Northcote House)

OFFICE FOR STANDARDS IN EDUCATION (1993), *Technology: Key Stages 1, 2 and 3: Second Year* (London: HMSO)

OFFICE FOR STANDARDS IN EDUCATION (1995), *Design and Technology: A Review of Inspection Findings* (London: HMSO)

OFFICE FOR STANDARDS IN EDUCATION (1996), *Subjects and Standards* (London: HMSO)

PEARCE, P. (1978), *The Battle of Bubble and Squeak* (London: Puffin)

PETERS, T. and AUSTIN, N. (1986), *A Passion for Excellence* (London: Fontana)

PIAGET, J. (1929), *The Child's Conception of the World* (London: Harcourt Brace)

RIDGEWELL, J. (1994), *Working with Food in Primary Schools* (London: Ridgewell Press)

RITCHIE, R. (1995), *Primary Design and Technology* (London: David Fulton)

ROSS, C. and BROWNE, N. (1993), *Girls as Constructors in the Early Years* (Stoke-on-Trent: Trentham Books)

RUSSELL, S. (1994), *Ready for Action: A Practical Guide to Post-Ofsted Action Planning* (Leamington Spa: Courseware Publications)

SCHOOLS CURRICULUM AND ASSESSMENT AUTHORITY (1994), *Design and Technology in the National Curriculum: Draft Proposals* (London: HMSO)

SCHOOLS CURRICULUM AND ASSESSMENT AUTHORITY (1996), *Nursery Education: Desirable Outcomes for Children's Learning* (London: SCAA)

SCHOOLS EXAMINATIONS AND ASSESSMENT COUNCIL (SEAC) (1992), *Technology Standard Assessment Tasks: Key Stage 1* (London: SEAC)

SCHOOLS EXAMINATIONS AND ASSESSMENT COUNCIL (SEAC) (1990), *Records of Achievement in Primary Schools* (London: HMSO)

SHEFFIELD, D. (1991), 'Getting started, primary data', *DATA*, Autumn

SIMON, B. (ed) (1993), *Education Answers Back: Critical Responses to Government Policy* (London: Lawrence and Wishart)

SIRAJ-BLATCHFORD, J. (1993), *Values in design and technology: beyond epistemology and ethnocentrism*, Paper presented to the International Conference on Design and Technology Education Research and Curriculum Development, Loughborough: UK

SMITHERS, A. and ROBINSON, P. (1992), *Getting it Right* (London: The Engineering Council)

THOMAS, J. (1972), *The Tay Bridge Disaster: New Light on the 1879 Tragedy* (Newton Abbot: David and Charles)

VULLIAMY, G. and WEBB, R. (1995), 'The implementation of the National Curriculum in small primary schools', *Educational Review*, **47**, 1

VYGOTSKY, L.S. (1962), *Thought and Language* (Massachusetts: Massachusetts Institute for Technology Press)

WEBB, R. (1990), *Practitioner Research in the Primary School* (London: The Falmer Press)

WEBB, R. (1993), *Eating the Elephant Bit by Bit* (London: Association of Teachers and Lecturers)

WHITE, E.B. (1952), *Charlotte's Web* (Harmondsworth: Puffin)

WILLIAMS, P. (1990), *Teaching Craft, Design and Technology* (London: Routledge)

WRAGG, E.C., BENNETT, N. and CARRE, C.G. (1989), 'Primary teachers and the National Curriculum', *Research Papers in Education*, **4**, 3, pp. 17–45

Index